The River Cottage

Curing & Smoking Handbook

The River Cottage
Curing & Smoking
Handbook

by Steven Lamb

with an introduction by
Hugh Fearnley-Whittingstall

www.rivercottage.net

BLOOMSBURY
LONDON · NEW DELHI · NEW YORK · SYDNEY

Ever since I first embarked on my River Cottage adventures, almost two decades ago, I've had the same aim: to bring myself and, with luck, those around me closer to the source of what we eat. That might mean something as simple as buying eggs from a neighbour rather than a supermarket, or learning how to joint a whole chicken rather than buying it in expensive portions. But I've derived huge pleasure and satisfaction from delving further into the realms of food production – growing my own vegetables, for instance, and raising my own livestock.

Such projects, though hugely enjoyable, are undeniably challenging and involve some commitment. I know they're not for everyone – or at least, not yet. But if you would like to give a bit less space to the middlemen and regain control, at least to some extent, over what you're feeding your family, then there are other elements of food production you can take into your own hands with amazing ease. Home-curing and smoking are among the most enticing.

These are techniques that take you one delicious step beyond your average recipe. They represent a deeper level of engagement with food than baking a cake or simmering a stew – perhaps because they require the deployment of often ancient artisan skills. These skills need not be daunting but they do set you off on a new learning curve. The cook who makes their own bacon enters a different arena from the one who roasts their own pork. And, correspondingly, he or she reaches a new level of gratification – often by no means instant, but always lasting.

Having said that, many of Steven's fantastic recipes are very straightforward and relatively quick. These dishes do a great deal to dismantle any mystique that surrounds home-curing – it is, at heart, a very simple procedure. Today we may think of these processes as being specialised and professional. But in times past everyone who raised livestock of any kind had a basic knowledge of how to use salt and smoke to help spread the goodness through the year. And everyone, whether rural smallholder or keen city cook, still can.

Of course, some of the items that Steven explores with such relish require more application than others – they are as much projects as recipes. They may take half a day to put together and a long time to mature – weeks, sometimes months. For some you will need to invest in specialist kit (a robust mincer, for example, and a sausage stuffer) or large quantities of ingredients (such as big cuts of meat or whole sacks of salt).

But the rewards for your dedication, for any extra outlay or time, are immense. Curing meat or smoking fish doesn't only result in a delicious end product; the gift is much greater than that. These are processes that unlock the secrets of some of our best-loved, most useful ingredients. They give you the keys to the citadel of smoky, salty-sweet-savoury moreishness: the hallowed place where bacon, air-dried ham, smoked salmon and kippers dwell. That may sound a bit over the top, but I stand

The River Cottage Curing & Smoking Handbook

by Steven Lamb

with an introduction by
Hugh Fearnley-Whittingstall

www.rivercottage.net

BLOOMSBURY
LONDON · NEW DELHI · NEW YORK · SYDNEY

For Elli, Aggie & Betsy

First published in Great Britain 2014

Text © 2014 by Steven Lamb
Photography © 2014 by Gavin Kingcome
Illustrations © 2014 by Toby Atkins

Bloomsbury Publishing Plc, 50 Bedford Square, London WC1B 3DP
Bloomsbury Publishing, London, New Delhi, New York and Sydney
www.bloomsbury.com

A CIP catalogue record for this book is available from the British Library

ISBN 978 1 4088 0882 5
10 9 8 7 6 5 4 3 2 1

Project editor: Janet Illsley
Designer: Will Webb
Photographer: Gavin Kingcome
Illustrator: Toby Atkins
Indexer: Hilary Bird

Printed and bound in Italy by Graphicom

www.bloomsbury.com/rivercottage

www.rivercottage.net

Contents

Tradition & Science   8

The Principles   18

Kit   40

Ingredients   56

The Methods   94

Recipes   134

Useful Things   246

Ever since I first embarked on my River Cottage adventures, almost two decades ago, I've had the same aim: to bring myself and, with luck, those around me closer to the source of what we eat. That might mean something as simple as buying eggs from a neighbour rather than a supermarket, or learning how to joint a whole chicken rather than buying it in expensive portions. But I've derived huge pleasure and satisfaction from delving further into the realms of food production – growing my own vegetables, for instance, and raising my own livestock.

Such projects, though hugely enjoyable, are undeniably challenging and involve some commitment. I know they're not for everyone – or at least, not yet. But if you would like to give a bit less space to the middlemen and regain control, at least to some extent, over what you're feeding your family, then there are other elements of food production you can take into your own hands with amazing ease. Home-curing and smoking are among the most enticing.

These are techniques that take you one delicious step beyond your average recipe. They represent a deeper level of engagement with food than baking a cake or simmering a stew – perhaps because they require the deployment of often ancient artisan skills. These skills need not be daunting but they do set you off on a new learning curve. The cook who makes their own bacon enters a different arena from the one who roasts their own pork. And, correspondingly, he or she reaches a new level of gratification – often by no means instant, but always lasting.

Having said that, many of Steven's fantastic recipes are very straightforward and relatively quick. These dishes do a great deal to dismantle any mystique that surrounds home-curing – it is, at heart, a very simple procedure. Today we may think of these processes as being specialised and professional. But in times past everyone who raised livestock of any kind had a basic knowledge of how to use salt and smoke to help spread the goodness through the year. And everyone, whether rural smallholder or keen city cook, still can.

Of course, some of the items that Steven explores with such relish require more application than others – they are as much projects as recipes. They may take half a day to put together and a long time to mature – weeks, sometimes months. For some you will need to invest in specialist kit (a robust mincer, for example, and a sausage stuffer) or large quantities of ingredients (such as big cuts of meat or whole sacks of salt).

But the rewards for your dedication, for any extra outlay or time, are immense. Curing meat or smoking fish doesn't only result in a delicious end product; the gift is much greater than that. These are processes that unlock the secrets of some of our best-loved, most useful ingredients. They give you the keys to the citadel of smoky, salty-sweet-savoury moreishness: the hallowed place where bacon, air-dried ham, smoked salmon and kippers dwell. That may sound a bit over the top, but I stand by it. Because, let's be honest, preserving and flavouring your own food in this way is pretty cool. If, like me, you love not just the finished dish but the process itself, then making a bacon butty with pork belly that you've cured yourself or whittling some wafer-thin slices from a leg of your very own air-dried ham represents a kind of culinary nirvana. It doesn't get much better.

These techniques are empowering. As Steven points out, once you've salted a whole piece of pork and successfully air-dried it in your own backyard, you'll feel no curing challenge is out of reach. You'll realise that you have the capacity to produce wholly authentic, traditional charcuterie – you are an artisan! And every time you follow one of the recipes in this book, your confidence will grow.

You're in very good hands here. Steven Lamb is an absolute linchpin of the whole River Cottage operation and has been for a decade. He and I go back to the early days, when River Cottage HQ was a scrubbed-out cow barn with a second-hand kitchen rammed into a shed next door. He's shared our learning curve from the off, assisting with our earliest efforts in curing and smoking and building his knowledge through experiment and experience. He is now our go-to guy for all things salty and smoky.

Steven's knowledge is as broad as it is deep. He currently guides River Cottage visitors through everything from building clay bread ovens to butchering pigs. But it's as the teacher on our meat curing and smoking courses that he has achieved guru status – with both his River Cottage colleagues and the many hundreds he has taught over the years. That's no surprise: quite apart from the fact that his coppa is, hands-down, the best I've ever tasted, Steven is relentlessly passionate about this subject. He has a never-ending fascination for charcuterie and salumi, for cures and brines, for the subtle interplay of salt, smoke and time. It's been a joy to see him pass this passion on to the people he teaches, and I'm thrilled he is now doing the same for readers of this brilliant book.

So, set aside any thoughts you may have about successful curing being beyond you. If you have some salt, pepper and sugar in your cupboard (or frankly, even just some salt!) you're ready to go. You can start experimenting now with a good strip of pork, or plump piece of fish. Next time, perhaps you'll add your own blend of herbs and spices to the cure, or you'll press an old biscuit tin into service as a hot-smoker to enhance that cured flesh even further. With this twanging new string to your culinary bow, you're well on your way to being a more versatile, accomplished and ultimately fulfilled cook.

Hugh Fearnley-Whittingstall, East Devon, January 2014

Tradition & Science

Real delicatessens are magical places.

By 'real', I mean stocked with authentic, artisan-made produce, independently run and, sadly, mostly abroad. For me, these places are the equivalent of the sweet shop to a young child or the church to a believer. I could spend an age looking at hams, sausages and salami, sizing up the interplay of ingredients, craftsmanship, culture and geography that goes to make each unique item. It is not unusual to find me staring wide-eyed in wonderment at an array of charcuterie, muttering under my breath about the possible methods used to get to the final results and mentally working backwards to their original source. I have the incurable River Cottage affliction of wanting to know the whole story of an ingredient, all the ins and outs of it, and I will pepper with questions whoever is on the other side of the counter in my bid to unlock the secrets. It is fair to say that I have an unholy reverence for cured produce.

My obsession actually stems from a rather unexpected place. As a young boy in the 1970s, my mother would stockpile tins of Pek Chopped Pork and find umpteen ways of serving it to my brother and me – especially, as I recall, when we were on holiday. Dozens of tins, placed in a box, would be the first thing packed into the car. My mother is a fantastic cook but despite her best intentions – and with a tight budget to feed us on – the experience was never less than awful. Whether it was given pride of place in a barm cake, scattered in a salad or fried and served with a pineapple hat, the stuff was always bland, tasteless and alien. We used to call it 'pet shop pork'. She had an inverted snobbery as far as it was concerned: it was never to be referred to as 'spam' because that was too common, a name that belittled the exotic nature of this versatile lump of pork in a tin from Poland.

Any interest I had in charcuterie might have been quashed by this early exposure to the bland, pretend end of it. Instead, I took the view that anything else would surely be an improvement. And so at every opportunity I would try any food that had its origins in the tradition of curing. I sampled corned beef and hams – cured in honey or molasses, brined, roasted and sliced wafer thin. I tasted salami rolled in black pepper, with chilli seeds that made me catch my breath, and cold-smoked salmon run through scrambled eggs on Christmas morning.

Everything was worth exploring and almost everything I tried I liked (with the exception of tripe with vinegar and onions). What began as an attempt to redress the balance for all the Pek Chopped Pork I had endured became an adventure, a journey. I felt myself becoming a little more sophisticated with each new taste, as if I was absorbing some of the culture and tradition behind the product as well as the flavours.

When holidays became slightly more elaborate and involved travelling abroad, I could hardly believe my luck. While everyone else was pulling faces at the sight of a Continental breakfast, I would be delighted at being given the chance to eat

Mortadella

Air-dried prosciutto

ham, pastrami, salami and smoked cheese first thing in the morning. The obsession grew – I wanted to experience the most authentic versions of cured foods. For a while, only produce on stalls in market squares in Spain, Italy and France, sold by the people who actually made it, would satisfy me.

The pinnacle of my tasting journey (so far) was not one of the big players, such as Ibérico or serrano ham, but a morsel of soppressata eaten in Tuscany, cut from a hanging salami barely a week old, spread on a slice of warm bruschetta by the owner of a small bar up in the hills. That might seem a bit cavalier to those of you with a keen sense of basic food hygiene, but I was caught up in the moment. And it was wonderful, a taste that seemed to encapsulate all the romance and tradition of curing and smoking.

However, I live in deepest Dorset, not in central Europe and although there are now some very good producers of both artisan and commercial cured products in this country, it was only a matter of time before I started to experiment with producing my own cured delicacies. And the results astounded me. I've been curing and smoking my own meats, fish and cheese for several years now and I have a passion for guiding other people who want to do the same.

Our European cousins have never lost the connection between food and culture, and they have allowed their curing and smoking traditions to thrive – a fact that makes me extremely happy but ever so slightly envious. Yet there's no reason why we shouldn't be enjoying our own fantastic smoked and cured produce here. We had the tradition in Britain but somehow forgot about it. Instead of passing on the expertise and recipes that our great-grandparents or great-great-grandparents would have known, we just stopped using them. But that disassociation is only in our heads. And I am glad to say that there are already some very fine new purveyors of this traditional craft breaking through, exploring afresh the methods that were part of our past. With this book, I'd like to be part of that resurgence.

It fills me with pleasure that both of my lovely young daughters have inherited the charcuterie gene. A recent trip to Spain saw them scoffing chorizo and chomping on morcilla like they were born to it. Why shouldn't we all? The age-old techniques of curing and smoking encompass craft, tradition, science and sorcery but, in looking towards the Continent for inspiration, I am constantly reminded how accessible and uncomplicated curing and smoking can be.

The straightforward, traditional methods laid out here will enable anyone to produce fantastic, authentic results. Creating simple cured products will expand your knowledge of food and increase your repertoire of dishes from all over the globe. It will enable you to take good British ingredients and turn them into elevated versions of themselves, applying minimum intervention. If you're curious, then I hope this book will be the beginning of your own wonderful journey of experimentation and reward.

A history of curing and smoking

Curing and smoking are deeply rooted in food history. They are among the earliest fundamental cooking techniques and can be traced back to ancient civilisations such as the Egyptians. Initially, they were the result of a need to make use of whatever food was available and extend its life so that communities could be sustained throughout the barren months. The process of curing food (through the application of salt), or of smoking it, has a dehydrating effect. In the days before refrigeration, this drying-out process was crucial for preserving food because it is moisture that fosters bacterial growth and leads to spoilage. Fortuitously, both salting and smoking have positive effects on flavour too.

Examples of traditional cured and smoked foods can be found throughout the world, in both sophisticated and apparently primitive societies. For example, the Japanese produce a seasoning called katsuobushi – tuna fillets air-dried, smoked intermittently over a month then left to ferment in the sun until they resemble wooden blocks covered in mould. Fine shavings are planed off and added to dishes as a topping, in a similar way to Parmesan. Meanwhile the Inuit people of Northern Greenland have a centuries-old method of preserving meat that produces something called kiviaq. Small Arctic birds called auks are stuffed into the fatty skin of a slaughtered seal, which is then sewn up, buried under rocks in the cold ground and left to ferment over a period of months before being eaten raw.

There is the intriguing question of how these methods came about in the first place. What made the first Inuit or Japanese person come to the conclusion that these processes would yield good results? It is impossible to know for sure but their significance is clear. Both of these examples were – and still are – efficient ways of preserving food over the harsh winter months, an effective response to the basic need to survive.

Trying conditions and a paucity of ingredients have never stood in the way of progress in the arts of curing and smoking. In fact, hardship and difficulty have been their very lifeblood, forcing invention and ingenuity. The processes have never been entirely fixed or locked down but rather they have evolved, with success coming as a result of a true understanding of what is available and the best way to use it.

In this way, the landscape, the seasons, local breeds, the diet available to the livestock and the weather itself have shaped different cured products from all over the world, and fixed them in their own particular places. Ibérico ham, for instance, which is one of the finest air-dried hams in the world, is only made from the pata negra ('black foot') pig in a specific part of Spain. And the best Ibérico comes from pigs fed on a diet of acorns from local oak-wood pastures. There is nothing else like it, which is part of its enduring appeal.

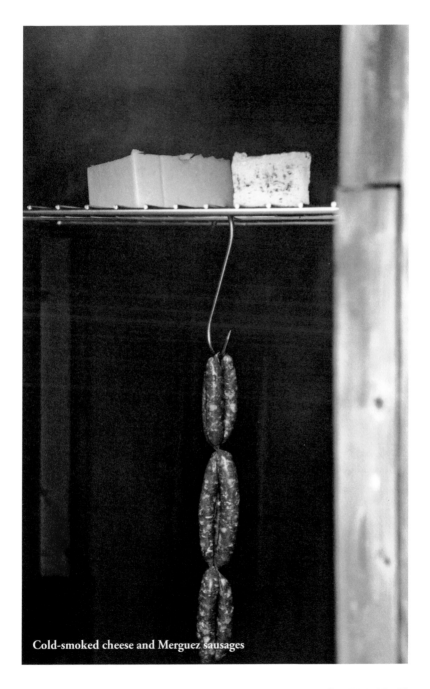

Cold-smoked cheese and Merguez sausages

Most of the recipes in this book illustrate the two main European styles of curing and smoking, charcuterie and salumi, although I have borrowed from Eastern European methods as well. As their names suggest, the recipes largely originate from either France or Italy. They rely on slightly different techniques, but follow the same fundamental principles – the differences between them are more to do with style and geographical origin than basic technique.

'Charcuterie' is a derivation of the French word *chair*, meaning 'flesh', and *cuit*, meaning 'cooked'. Originally, charcuterie was used solely as a term to describe preserved pork products, but it now encompasses products made from a wider selection of meats. Traditional charcuterie items include confit, sausages, pâtés, terrines and hams.

'Salumi' is the Italian word used to describe any cured or smoked meat, such as salami, prosciutto, coppa, guanciale or bresaola.

There are also recipes here for bacon, ham and smoked fish – great cured products that stem from our own British curing tradition. Home-made bacon, as it happens, is one of the very best recipes with which to begin your own curing adventure (see pp.138–43).

Both the Continental and British styles of curing draw on very old, traditional culinary methods, and there are various rules that should be adhered to – more on that later. But what excites me about them is that, within the confines of each method, there is room for you to exercise a little individuality and introduce the ingredients that suit your palate. Curing and smoking continue to evolve with every generation and the minute you decide to make your first bit of home-cured bacon, you become part of the story. As well as drawing from the tradition, your own experience adds to it.

Traditional cured foods

As with most artisan-made things, there is a threat to the existence of traditional cured foods. While most of these crafts are still practised in the original way at least somewhere, the majority of them are also replicated using more commercial methods. For every authentic cured product, there is an antithesis: a factory-made, mass-produced alternative that usually bears the same name but few or none of the original qualities.

The fast-food, accelerated version of smoking and curing culture is perhaps now the most prominent. By which I mean if you go and buy any of the classic cured products, such as air-dried ham, salami or bacon, the chances are you will get a mass-produced version. This is even true in Italy and France, the homes of salumi and charcuterie.

This is of course the way of the world, but it makes me uneasy. Even the most well-intentioned large-scale manufacturers, who want to make something very good, have to think about their bottom line. Generally, mass-production eradicates the hard-won collective knowledge that led to a product's original identity. It kills off the craft because factories need to churn out large volumes – quickly and cheaply. There is no room for the practice of patience.

However, the news is not all bad – far from it. In many parts of Europe, while the commercial machine has trundled on inexorably, it hasn't steam-rollered all the traditional producers in the process. In Britain more and more traditional producers are appearing, although they still account for just 1% of the charcuterie and salumi consumed here. The original crafts have remained and, in some places, flourished. In fact, these are good times for lovers of cured foods, as long as you are discerning.

More and more cured products are protected by laws that uphold their quality and authenticity. PDO status (Protected Designation of Origin), attached to products such as prosciutto, culatello and lardo, is becoming more widespread. The recently launched New Nordic Food Movement, for instance, has captured the collective imagination, as well as political support, in and around Scandinavia. It manages to promote local, traditional foods while delivering at a modern, commercial level by helping small producers supply top-end restaurants such as Noma in Copenhagen. Similarly, in Italy, the Slow Food Movement has protected traditional products from an influx of foreign fast-food alternatives, and now has charitable status.

It won't come as any surprise to read that I am a champion of the traditional, old-fashioned approach. I want it to be a continuation and reflection of the skilled craftsmanship that inspired me in the first place and, for that reason, I have the home-curing enthusiast, rather than the commercial operator, in mind here.

I do not, however, mean to denigrate anyone who wants to try curing or smoking on a commercial scale. Nor do I think being commercially successful is synonymous with the abandonment of tradition. I have included some very fine producers local to me in Dorset (see the Directory, p.248), who manage to balance the commercial and the artisan. But there are important considerations to take on board. Anyone who prepares cured foods needs to think about the nature of their ingredients, but the commercial processor must also adhere to the regulations and recommendations from the Environmental Health Office (EHO), Food Standards Agency (FSA) and Trading Standards that relate to selling food (see pp.36–9).

e Principles

In order to start curing and smoking, it is important to understand the basic science behind the techniques and how the main ingredients interact to flavour and preserve.

Fresh meat does not have a very long shelf life. Once it stops being part of a living animal it begins to deteriorate under the influence of enzymes, oxygen and light. This process is not entirely negative: it can improve texture as well as flavour, as in the example of aged beef. However, ultimately, meat that is left unadulterated will spoil.

Bacteria thrive on the surface of meat and will multiply infinitely if you let them, while the moisture and fats break down over time and turn the meat rancid. (Meats that carry a higher percentage of saturated fat, such as beef or pork, take longer to spoil than those with more unsaturated fat, such as poultry or fish.) In curing and smoking, we are applying ingredients and creating conditions that either arrest deterioration or control the process so that it can happen safely over an extended period.

The key to curing successfully is the reduction or eradication of moisture in meat. This creates an environment that is not only inhospitable to the bacteria that cause products to spoil and 'go off' but, crucially, beneficial for microbes that protect the meat and add flavour. For, as well as preventing the growth of the unwelcome bacteria that cause spoilage, we actually want to attract specific bacteria, namely halophiles (meaning 'salt-lovers').

These beneficial bacteria thrive in dry, salty conditions. When in contact with meat, they create lactic acid, which both protects the meat from pathogenic bacteria such as listeria, and encourages desirable moulds such as *Penicillium*, which will also work to your advantage. If salt is used in the right way, the food will become stable. Over time, it will continue to dry out and, eventually, it will get too hard to eat, but it will never go off.

Smoking complements salting. Smoke of course adds a spectrum of complex flavours that can enhance a huge range of ingredients but it also has a preservative effect. Phenol, a compound within smoke, acts as an antioxidant which inhibits the rancidification of fat, while naturally occurring formaldehyde and acetic acid lower the pH (increase the acidity) when deposited on the surface of meat, fish or poultry, which has an anti-microbial effect.

Salted meat

Salt and fat

Curing is a layer of love applied to something that you already hold a deep affection for. And it is the crucial ingredients – salt and fat – that really fuel the affair. Of course there are health issues related to these key players. However, those issues are connected to consuming them in excess. Granted, if you ate nothing but bacon, chorizo and ham, you would have cause for concern, but modest quantities of home-cured produce, consumed as part of a balanced diet, can be enjoyed without anxiety.

When you read through some of my recipes, you may be surprised at some of the quantities of salt and fat listed. But please remember those are the quantities needed to successfully preserve that particular ingredient, which may be a very large piece of meat. When you sit down to eat a portion of it, you will only be consuming a tiny fraction of the original salt and fat.

Salt

In all curing and preserving methods there is one common denominator: sodium chloride. This is just ordinary, everyday salt. However, used in the right way, it is a truly miraculous substance. If all the ingredients known to man were lined up against a wall in preparation for the biggest imaginable 'cook off' of all time, I would pick out salt first and make it my team captain.

Sodium chloride is, quite literally, the salt of the earth, a primeval mineral, released by the natural erosion of rocks in the world's oceans or mined from deep underground. Much attention is given to the dangers of consuming too much salt and of course we should all be mindful of our intake. But salt is most harmful when it is hidden – as it is in many commercially processed foods – so that you can be consuming excessive amounts without realising it.

It is easy to forget that salt is nevertheless essential – a nutrient our bodies cannot do without. Nerve and muscle cells (including those in the heart) generate electrical energy by creating an imbalance of sodium across a cell membrane. If a body is deficient in sodium it struggles to do this, leading to muscle weakness and neurological problems.

Salt is also unbelievably useful when used wisely: it has been employed for thousands of years, across every geographical region on earth, to enhance food and extend its natural life. Salt has travelled through time with us, seasoning and preserving what we eat.

Salt can be applied to food to suppress flavours as well as enhance them. It elevates natural tastes and aromas but also softens bitterness. It is a mineral that has been the basis of survival for many of the ancient civilisations we deem to be advanced, such as the Egyptians and Romans. It has even been used as a currency, particularly on trading routes in the ancient world. It was also known as 'white gold'. A Roman soldier's pay was called *salarium*, from the Latin *sal* for 'salt', because the soldiers used it to buy salt; our word 'salary' comes from this. Salt remains central in just about every kitchen across the planet.

The preservative ability of salt stems from its unique molecular structure. It is comprised of small, highly concentrated, super-busy, positively and negatively charged atoms that penetrate other foods. Salt draws out moisture, which limits the growth of the microbes that cause meat to spoil. The salt itself then travels in the opposite direction, into the meat, and promotes the benign bacteria that bring flavour. This subtle, gradual exchange is known as osmosis and it happens to be one of my favourite transactions related to food.

By drastically slowing down deterioration, salt creates a window of opportunity for flavour to develop. Within the meat, enzymes digest natural sugars and then release lactic or acetic acid (an enzyme is, in essence, a substance produced by a living organism that acts as a catalyst to bring about a biochemical reaction). These acids in turn break down proteins and fats into smaller molecules, such as peptides. Over the course of several weeks or months, peptides convert into a complex array of flavoursome compounds with citrus and nutty notes.

As well as drawing out moisture and drying the meat, therefore starving and killing off unwanted micro-organisms (and imparting flavour), salt also alters its texture and appearance. A concentration of salt loosens the protein strands in the muscle cells, which are usually grouped together tightly, causing them to separate. This weakens the fibres, which gives cured meats a silky tenderness and slightly translucent appearance.

You'll find information about the specific types of salt I recommend for use in curing and smoking on pp.82–3.

Fat

Although often talked about as a single, malign entity, there are many different kinds of fat, some of which are known to be beneficial when consumed in the right quantities. There are fats, or rather elements of fat, such as omega-3 and omega-6 fatty acids which are considered essential but on the whole, should you choose to, you could probably survive without consuming fat in your diet. It would, however, be a miserable culinary experience and I, for one, would never choose to do that. Fat is where flavour resides and it is a fantastic commodity in both domestic and commercial kitchens.

Fat was an everyday ingredient to me, growing up. Beef dripping had pride of place in the pantry and my dad would spread it on everything, like a master plasterer at work. In our house, pork crackling could start a fight. My mum kept a frying pan of fat constantly on the go: it was used for every breakfast, placed on

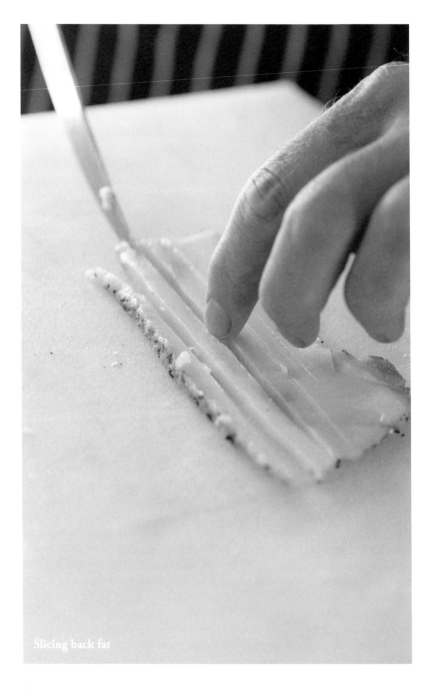

Slicing back fat

the stove top until the solid fat had rendered down and started to spit. At that point, bacon would be placed into the hot fat, followed by eggs and bread. Once the cooking had been completed it would be put to the back of the stove and allowed to cool and set again ready for the next time. It was a magic pan that never lost any of its contents and woke from its solid creamy white slumber to become clear and liquid over and over again. I loved that battered, blue-handled, fat-filled pan and expect it to be bequeathed to me when my mum is ready to hand it on, our one family heirloom.

I realise that some of you reading this are likely to be appalled! We have been encouraged to cut down on fat, and animal fats in particular – the very fats, as it happens, that are most useful in the curing process. We are constantly informed that eating fat causes high cholesterol, which will ultimately lead to heart disease. But it is a common misconception that all animal fats are saturated and that all are bad for you.

Our consumption of animal fats cannot be blamed entirely for the alarming increase in obesity levels, high cholesterol and related health problems. Over the last 60 years or so, the population as a whole has become much less active and the quality of our diets has deteriorated, with too much reliance on overly processed food, especially cheap high-energy sugary foods and drinks.

Traditional fats such as lard and butter have been demonised and 'healthier' alternatives such as margarine and vegetable oils have flooded the shelves, but these are not necessarily healthier options – margarine, in particular, is a source of harmful 'trans-fats'. Perhaps it is time we took a more balanced view on animal fats. It is, after all, a case of moderation.

Avoiding animal fats not only robs us of flavour, it has also meant that animal husbandry and breeding practices have changed for the worse. As consumers, we have become suspicious of visible fat left on meat; we assume it's there to add weight and cost. Animals are therefore bred to be leaner these days. The introduction of large white pigs in this country almost killed off the traditional, slow-growing breeds that put flavoursome layers of fat on top of wonderful meat – they are now called rare breeds for a reason.

In addition, when flavour is seen as less important than leanness, the conditions in which animals are kept generally deteriorate. Living in cramped quarters without access to natural light, and unable to indulge in all their natural behaviours, they are not allowed to mature properly, and this is reflected in the lack of fat and flavour in the meat that they produce.

The use of fat – pork fat in particular – is crucial in the curing process, not least because it keeps the flavour and texture in your meat while it loses moisture. On p.81 you will find more about the specific types of fat that are used. I, for one, will continue to enjoy fat, in sensible quantities, without qualms.

Bacteria

The processes of curing and smoking can be understood on one level as the introduction and rebuffing of bacteria and moulds. These may not be particularly appetising terms, which is why the marketing industry uses words like 'ageing' and 'maturing' to describe the effects of these micro-organisms. It is more appealing to talk about 'well-hung beef', for instance, than 'decomposing flesh'. Similarly, moulds may be described as 'benign blooms' which dust the surface of meat or cheese, though it would be equally accurate to describe them as 'incubating' and 'multiplying' micro-organisms.

At the end of the day, it all boils down to the same thing: a controlled ageing process. And, whichever way you choose to phrase it, when it comes to home-curing, you are the agent of that control, the first and last line of defence – the head of security at the microbe club.

Bacteria, like it or not, are already playing an active, if invisible, role in your daily life. They are present in every environment and our bodies house hundreds of different types. There are probably at least 100 different bacteria on this page alone and many more on the skin of your hand. Bacteria are particularly prominent in food, and especially in cured, uncooked meat, so you can see why you need to develop a fine understanding of their positive and negative qualities.

In fact, very few bacteria are working against us. On the whole, they perform an important role in keeping us ticking over, helping us to digest and metabolise food. Any bad bacteria are generally dealt with by our immune system but there are some that you simply don't want to meet.

Rather like basic, minute single-cell versions of humans, bacteria consume food, create waste and reproduce. Bacteria are most active in a warm environment (between 26 and 35°C) and like a wet situation – so they are partial, for instance, to water or blood.

Raw meat is high in water – up to 80% – and therefore a favourable place for bacteria, which, in the right conditions, will multiply quickly. The level of liquid present in raw meat is crucial in the curing process: too much liquid promotes bad bacterial growth and makes the meat 'turn' or go off. The application of salt – and also, to some extent, cold smoke – is a key way in which we reduce the water content in meat and thereby preserve it. When salt is applied to meat it creates a high concentration of dissolved sodium and chloride ions within the meat. The water inside the muscle cells is drawn out because of the effect of osmolarity, or pressure, and the salt is absorbed.

Additionally, in very high-salt solutions, such as wet-cure brines, many microbes will rupture, owing to the difference in pressure between the outside and inside of the organism. Most bacteria, with the exception of the beneficial halophiles ('salt-loving' bacteria), cannot grow in conditions where the level of salt is greater than 3%. Solutions with a high concentration of sugar have the same effect on microbes, which is why sugar is used as a preservative in jams and jellies, and also in a basic dry cure or brine.

Salt also increases acidity, lowering the pH in the meat and making it less hospitable to microbes that cause spoilage. The perfect pH in cured meat is 4.5–5, which inhibits unwanted bacterial growth but allows benign white powdery moulds and airborne yeasts to spore on the surface. These contribute additional flavours by denaturing the bacterial acids on the surface, giving dry-cured, air-dried meat that tangy, aromatic flavour.

The wrong types of bacteria not only create sour or 'off' flavours, they can cause illness and, in the very worst-case scenario, death. So there is no place for a cavalier attitude with curing. The chances of contracting an illness from food-borne bacteria are minimal but that is no reason to stick your head in the sand. General good hygiene and correctly applied curing techniques should eliminate unwanted bacterial activity. But some curing methods, such as fermentation in the making of salami, are carried out within a potentially hazardous temperature range and the finished product is then eaten uncooked, which adds to the risk, so additional care must be taken. These are the areas of curing where the potential use of artificial anti-bacterial substances – namely nitrates, nitrites and starter cultures – comes to the fore.

Bacteria are not visible to the eye and therefore you cannot see if any negative bacteria are present. Of course, if a salami or cured ham leg was dripping black liquid and smelling awful, you could determine that it wasn't in the best shape to eat. However, bad bacteria don't always present themselves in such an obvious way. That is why it is important to be precise with measurements and careful about curing conditions: these are your only ways of controlling the cure (if you decide not to add nitrates and starter cultures).

Moulds

Just as there are good and bad bacteria, there are desirable and undesirable moulds. However, moulds are a slightly less scary subject because they are mostly benign (there is little or no risk that the wrong mould will kill you), and they are visible to the naked eye. Also, moulds grow at a much slower rate than bacteria (which, in the right conditions, can multiply into the millions from a standing start in under 10 hours).

With moulds, there is a greater element of control. They are only ever present on the surface of foods because they are aerobic (require oxygen) and so they

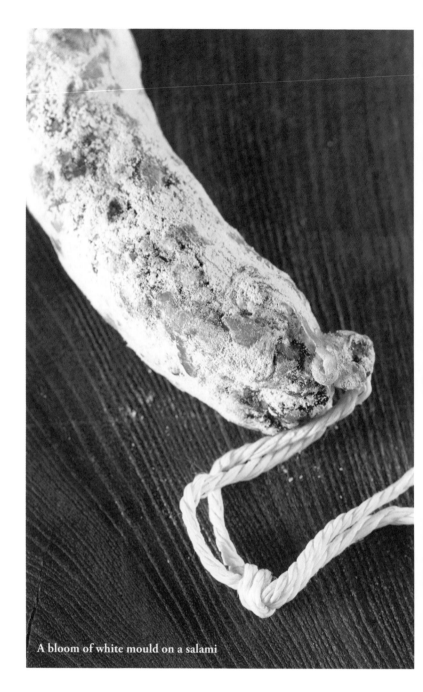

A bloom of white mould on a salami

cannot hide unnoticed in the middle of a salami. In extreme cases, you can get moulds that release poisonous 'mycotoxins' – but these tend to affect only grains or vegetables.

In most curing, the desired mould is a very distinct chalky-white variety known as *Penicillium*. This is similar to the blue mould you find in some cheeses (which is deliberately placed there by the cheesemaker). Not only does it contribute to the overall flavour of the cured product, it also performs three very important functions. Firstly, once the mould is present on the surface, it will grow to cover the entire surface, thereby inhibiting any harmful bacteria from getting a foothold. Secondly, it consumes oxygen and thereby reduces the process of oxidation in the cured product itself. Oxidation discolours and causes 'off flavours'. Lastly, it forms a barrier between the surface of the cured product and the natural light which can turn fat rancid.

Quite often, you'll come across other moulds on your cured foods – green, orange or black – and sometimes in fuzzy long fronds. These undesirable moulds are due mostly to an absence of air movement around the curing meat or too much warmth. Stagnant air generally causes the wrong moulds because the humidity levels are too high. Perfect air-drying humidity levels are between 60 and 80%, where the benevolent *Penicillium* moulds prosper.

However, these unwelcome moulds do not indicate that the meat is off (not unless it is actually black and dripping, with a rancid smell!). You can clean off unwanted moulds with a cloth or nail brush dampened in malt vinegar. This has anti-microbial qualities and will also increase the acidity on the surface of the food, which tends to promote the *Penicillium* mould that you want.

If you don't find the right mould growing on your cured meats, you can put it there yourself. You can buy a commercial culture, dissolve it in distilled water then apply the solution to the meat, or simply dip the meat into it. These cultures are available online from butcher's sundries websites (see Directory, p.248).

Alternatively, you can hang inexpensive shop-bought salami next to one of your own curing salami and the mould will simply travel from the finished product to your own. What's more, the beneficial microflora will then always be present in the area that you have designated as your air-drying spot for curing, which is a very good thing.

I have seen moulds of all types on cured food – both home-made and commercial products. My inbox is full of pictures of mouldy meat from all over the world! The rule of thumb should be to use the vinegar technique to clean off any mould that doesn't look powdery and white, check temperatures and humidity levels regularly and wait for the mould to come back in the desirable form. This will not harm the curing process – it just means that the flavour won't be as mature until the mould is present.

Nitrates and nitrites

You will have heard, I am sure, of a potentially fatal disease called botulism. This very nasty illness is caused by toxins released by *Clostridium botulinum* bacteria. Botulism is rare but, of course, it has to be taken very seriously. The *Clostridium botulinum* bacterium is found in soil and in aquatic sediments all over the globe. It remains dormant and unthreatening unless its environment becomes warm, moist, low in acidity and oxygen-free. The bacteria themselves are not harmful, but the toxins they produce are highly poisonous. The bacteria can be killed by cooking at a high temperature for a significant time. Most cases of food-borne botulism are caused by food being kept at the wrong temperature or being badly stored, or through bad practice at commercial canning factories.

Although good hygiene and correct technique should ensure that botulism is never able to take a hold, there is one way to be absolutely sure, and that is by using nitrates and nitrites in curing. It is the belt-and-braces way of eradicating this baddie and is viewed as a necessity in most commercial meat-curing operations. However, some artisan producers choose not to utilise these chemical compounds because they are not natural additives.

The use of nitrates and nitrites is a subject that often splits opinion, not just among producers, but also among scientists and physicians. I would like to help you navigate through this tricky subject. I don't use synthetic cures myself but I want you to make up your own mind.

The nitrates and nitrites commonly used in commercially cured meat products are found in pre-prepared mixes of curing salts, which may be called 'insta-cure', 'Prague powders' or 'pink salt'. (Most cure mixes are coloured pink to prevent accidental ingestion; however, the pink colour of Himalayan salt is naturally occurring.) These synthetic cures (sodium nitrate and sodium nitrite) are produced by chemical reaction. The salt is prepared in a lab, by treating sodium hydroxide with mixtures of nitrogen dioxide and nitric oxide:

$$2\ NaOH + NO_2 + NO \rightarrow 2\ NaNO_2 + H_2O$$

Commercial curing salts are mostly divided into two categories, often referred to as 'Cure #1' and 'Cure #2'.

Cure #1 This is a mixture of sodium nitrite (6.25%) and sodium chloride (93.75%). It is primarily used for curing whole muscle products that are to be cold-smoked, such as bacon. It is inadvisable to use nitrite-only cures, like Cure #1, in recipes that require a lengthy curing time because the nitrite gets used up (metabolised) relatively quickly.

Cure #2 This is a mixture of sodium nitrite (6.25%), sodium nitrate (4%) and sodium chloride (89.75%). It provides fast-acting protection against botulism from the nitrite, and a slower-release protection from the sodium nitrate. Cure #2 is used in salami that are to be cured over a long time. It should never be used on any product that will be fried at high temperatures, such as bacon, because of the resulting formation of nitrosamines (see overleaf).

There is another product, called 'Tender Mix', comprising 0.5% sodium nitrite and 0.5% sodium nitrate as well as sodium chloride, sugar and propylene glycol (used to keep the mix uniform). It is used primarily in the making of commercial brines.

Nitrates slowly react with naturally occurring bacteria, and are converted into nitrites. Nitrites are then converted to nitric oxide. This raises the acidity levels which help prevent meat from spoiling. However, acidity levels are raised effectively just by adding salt, which also produces lactic acid, adding a tangy piquancy that nitrate-treated products lack.

Nitric oxide combines with myoglobin – the pigment that makes meat red – to form nitrosomyoglobin, which fixes a deep-red colour in uncooked dry sausage. Without nitrites, cured meat doesn't always retain the original colour. For example, it is virtually impossible to replicate the pinkness of a commercial slice of corned beef without using the colour-fixing properties of nitrites.

Nitrites also act on the fibres of whole muscles of meat, giving them firmness and a slight sheen. This effect used to fuel my concerns about using nitrites because I thought they might possibly have the same effect on my physiology. (I could do with it in some areas but you don't have that control!) In fact, most of the nitrites are excreted from the body well before they have any effect on muscle tissue.

Adding nitrates as part of the curing process is not a new thing. Potassium nitrate (saltpetre) was used as early as the fifteenth century and, although it is viewed a little negatively these days (because of its other use, in explosives), it is still available and used throughout Europe. However, most producers use lab-prepared sodium nitrate.

It is possible to create safe, authentic cured products without the use of nitrates and nitrites. We've been doing it at River Cottage for a long time and this tradition is widespread throughout Europe. In order to ensure safety of the finished product, the most important factors are to get the temperature, humidity and acidity correct at all times (particularly during the fermentation process of making salami). Using good-quality raw materials and applying strict hygiene controls are also crucial.

Although nitrates and nitrites are added to many commercially cured foods, it is only really necessary for them to be added to meat that has been minced for making salami, in order to stop pathogenic bacteria growing. Botulism bacteria cannot grow on the exterior surface of meat but could thrive within the airless interior of salami, which is cured and dried at, or around, normal room temperature. One of the main beneficial qualities of nitrates and nitrites is that they function within the same temperature range at which bad bacteria thrive (26–35°C), and over a long period, so their use allows products such as salami to be cured for 6–8 weeks, unrefrigerated, free from any risk of botulism.

You can, however, cure salami at home without added nitrates or nitrites by applying the correct amount of salt. The minimum amount of salt required is 2%. If you then follow the procedures on p.103 and hang salami in the perfect drying conditions you will have no need for synthetic cure powders.

If you want to make salami-style products and you're in any doubt about your own environment or processes, I suggest you apply the recommended amounts of synthetic cures containing nitrates and nitrites. The minimum level of synthetic cure mix is 2.5g for every 1kg meat (in addition to conventional salt, of course).

So why don't I use these synthetic cures? Put simply, they are antithetical to my approach, which is to use the most natural ingredients and the most traditional methods that I can. Also, pure sodium nitrite is quite toxic to humans.

In addition, there are major concerns regarding the carcinogenic properties of nitrates, particularly when they are exposed to high temperatures – as when bacon is cooked. This can create compounds called nitrosamines, which can potentially cause cancer. Opinion is split on the precise levels required for such a devastating effect, although it is unlikely that the amount of nitrates used in commercially cured and processed meat is unsafe to this degree.

There is another dilemma here for anyone wanting to follow the authentic, natural route because although all of the above nitrite and nitrate mixes categorically stop pathogenic bacteria from forming and therefore remove the risk of botulism, they also introduce an element of the non-organic to your product. There are some synthetic cures on the market that are advertised as 'organic' but none come with a regulated stamp of approval from the Soil Association.

I have to concede, though, that nitrates and nitrites do also occur naturally. You find them in green vegetables such as spinach and celery. In fact, our metabolism frequently converts nitrates into nitrites as part of digestion: while the majority of them are excreted in our urine, some remain in the acidic environment of our stomachs, aiding digestion.

There are other, natural alternatives to commercial cure mixes, such as celery salt. The celery plant needs a soil high in nitrogen to thrive, and its seeds are rich in nitrates. These can be substituted for synthetic sodium nitrate in meat curing and have the same effect on salami as a synthetic nitrate. Celery extracts have very little pigment and a mild taste that does not detract from the flavour of the meat. They may be listed as natural flavourings on product labels. In addition, celery salt also contains high levels of antioxidants, which help your body process the nitrates.

PDV salt

Ham hock and brine bin

The downside to using celery salt, and it is a considerable downside, is that there is absolutely no way of regulating, or even knowing, how much nitrate it contains. So, even if you use the same amount of celery salt in every salami cure you make, the amount of nitrate present could vary dramatically. Celery salt is not for me because its use involves sheer guesswork.

Salt naturally contains nitrates and nitrites as well as a myriad of other minerals. Even though they occur in lower amounts than in synthetic cures, the action of salt in the right amounts has the same, if not superior, effect.

The decision as to whether or not to use nitrates or nitrites is a difficult one, particularly if you want to create traditional, authentic salami and cold-smoked products. There are certainly strong arguments for and against. Suffice to say, though, that at River Cottage, we do not add any nitrites or nitrates to our cured food. We do not believe you need them, as long as you follow best practice, add the right percentage of salt and keep the curing products in the right conditions.

We follow traditional methods, ones that are governed and championed by the likes of the Slow Food Movement, but have the advantage of modern scientific knowledge. We can apply precisely the correct ratio of salt and monitor pH levels (low acidity being a critical factor in the development of botulism), as well as air-drying in the best conditions so that humidity and temperature are perfect.

Bear in mind, also, that it is only really for fermented sausages, salami and items that are to be cold-smoked that the question of nitrates and nitrites comes up at all. You could stick to air-dried hams, unsmoked bacon and coppa and avoid the issue altogether.

Every cure is different

No matter how much I learn about the science of curing, it has never lessened for me the romance and excitement of it. One of the things I love about this craft (and this can be seen as an advantage of not using synthetic cure mixes) is that you will always find a subtle difference between every cured product you create. This is what I think of as the sorcery of curing, by which I mean the magic worked on a product by the unique ingredients that go into it and the environment in which it is made.

So, for instance, although I always make salami in essentially the same way, I still know that when I slice into a new one, it will be slightly, subtly different to the last. I love this element of the unknown, which sets every product apart and is really the final celebration of the process. If you have followed the method, used the key ingredients in the correct ratios and allowed the process to happen in the appropriate conditions, then this revelation of the unknown will always be a pleasant surprise and will engage the senses in new ways.

Commercial considerations

The main difference between domestic and commercial production of cured foods is the legal requirement to use non-natural preservatives containing sodium nitrites and sodium nitrates. If you do not use these, then your home-cured products should only be for home consumption or consumption amongst friends, family and 'general extended parties'. You are not permitted to sell them commercially unless you have a very sympathetic, understanding and progressive local Trading Standards Officer.

One key step, should you want to embark on a commercial operation, is to get the local Trading Standards Office and Environmental Health Office on your side and working with you from the outset. So many people enter into the commercial production process with the idea already formed that these bodies are there to be prohibitive. This simply isn't true or helpful.

In some cases, Trading Standards and Environmental Health Officers may not fully understand what you are trying to do, particularly if you are hoping to stick closely to traditional, artisan methods. But that just makes it doubly important for you to convey, at the earliest opportunity, the importance of traditional methods to your business – without, of course, sounding as if you have a total disregard for health and safety law. In short, get them to understand your business plan and your reasoning.

You will need to know about HACCPs (Hazard Analysis Critical Control Points). These are protocols for the production, storing and selling of produce – in effect, they are a set of operational guidelines which also act as a risk assessment system so that at any given point, from production to sale, there is an audit trail and accountability. These guidelines are written by you with the help of the Trading Standards and Environmental Health Officers, so that you can actively show them your high standards.

If you engage in the monitoring process willingly then, depending on individual local office compliance, you should be able to create a set of standards that are applicable to your own operation and may act as a pioneering template for other people's future businesses. Try to view this (admittedly not exciting) administrative task for what it is: vital work that enhances your operation because it shows good working practice.

Commercial food preparation standards

The correct handling of high risk areas can mean the difference between a successful business, run with the consent of the local Food Standards Agency/Environmental Health Office, and one that runs illegally that could potentially poison a customer. All of the risk areas are controllable; they simply require common sense.

Personal hygiene Have a designated hand-wash area and always wash your hands with anti-bacterial soap.

Meat Never allow cooked, cured and raw meats to come into contact with each other. Use separate areas and machinery for each item. Colour coding of equipment such as knives and chopping boards is an industry standard practice.

Working area As well as complying with the obvious points about hygiene, your working area should be clearly defined and reflect what you look to produce.

Handling Any area that is used for processing or handling raw meat should have a cutting zone with all the kit, such as meat mincers, sausage stuffers, slicers and wrapping tables.

Chopping surfaces You should have a balance of both wooden chopping surfaces and stainless-steel worktops.

Cold storage and freezing These should be separate areas. It could be as simple as a fridge and a freezer but it is unlikely that this would be sufficient for a business looking to process a number of different products. The cold storage would normally comprise an area or a walk-in unit that is chilled to 3°C, with a rail that large pieces of raw meat could be hung from, and a similar-sized freezer unit with clearly labelled stacking shelves.

Dry-curing areas If you want to have a designated dry-curing area then you can consider a commercial unit, of which there are some on the market that tick all the right boxes. These professional models can be set for the appropriate temperature, humidity and circulation of air with the capacity to cure salami or prosciutto at the touch of a button. They are also 'reassuringly' expensive (see Directory, p.248). If one of these units is a little out of your reach, then you need to create another separate area where you can control and maintain the range of temperatures, humidity and air movement that will suit the product, as well as conform to the HACCP guidelines. This area should really operate at a temperature in the range of 10–22°C, with a humidity level of 60–80% and with a system to circulate air. Buying a good thermo-hygrometer will enable you to measure humidity accurately (see p.54).

Labelling You always need to be clear about labelling the product for sale. You must have your business head in place so that your products are priced competitively, as well as reflect the effort and length of time it takes to get them to point of sale.

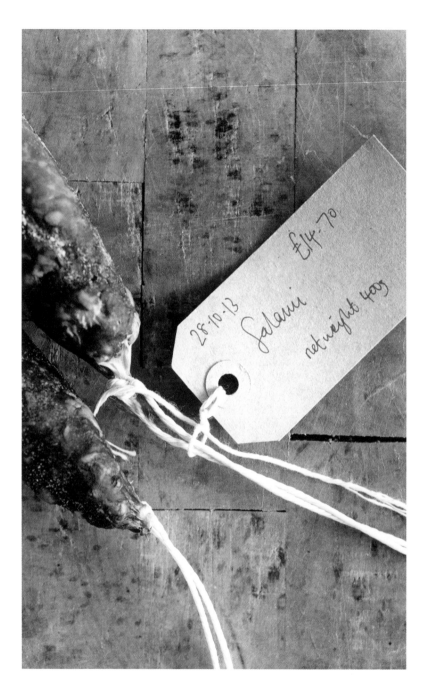

Information on packaging Products that are packaged have to carry a labelling system showing the ingredients, net weight, use-by date and price.

Testing Finally, although it is not a legal requirement, it is good working practice to send, willingly and unprompted, one or two randomly chosen products to be lab-tested for anything that might be considered harmful or dangerous. It is widely understood that cured meat products innately carry more than their fair share of bacteria and micro-organisms but of course the majority of them are encouraged or even introduced on purpose to benefit the process and final product. It is these positive bacteria that produce the unique taste and texture. However, the harmful bacteria which can occur through poor hygiene, incorrect handling and lack of diligence and common sense could actually kill you. There is no place at all for health-and-safety roulette.

In accordance with the information given by the Food Standards Agency, a good HACCP-based food-safety management system should:

- Be integral to the business; all members of staff should understand the requirements and what they have to do
- Be tailor-made to the needs of the business
- Include procedures for all food activities
- Have procedures that are simple yet comprehensive.

Kit

I have never been one for stockpiling shiny new equipment: it always seems to over-promise. Rather than empowering me, an abundance of appliances just makes me feel swamped and weighed down. This slight kit phobia is something that I have had to address as I've explored the world of curing and smoking. But rest assured, I still rarely do anything by machine that can be done as well by hand, and I will not be trying to persuade you to spend an arm and a leg on gadgets and gizmos.

As a home-curing enthusiast, there may be some things you just cannot do without, but you need far less stuff and far less space than a commercial operator would, and your initial investment should be fairly minimal. Before spending any money, consider what you hope to produce and in what quantities, and always think about storage space. Aim to buy just the items of equipment you need to start off your home-curing venture.

As with most things, there is a close relationship between cost and quality when it comes to buying this sort of equipment. You shouldn't have to spend a small fortune but the old adage of 'buy cheap, buy twice' does usually apply. Occasionally, there are exceptions that prove this rule, such as the old Victorian hand-cranked mincer I picked up at a local car-boot sale for a couple of quid which has never let me down. It can be worth shopping around a little. But generally the best place to look for the essential bits of kit is a butcher's sundries shop or website (see Directory, p.248). Often, you will find a 'one-stop shop', set up to supply both the commercial sector and the home enthusiast, which should be able to meet all your needs.

Machinery

If you are going to be making your own cured goods on a regular basis you will certainly need to invest in some machinery. You can always chop meat into coarse morsels with a sharp knife or slice relatively thin rashers off a cured piece of streaky bacon. You could, after a fashion, improvise with a funnel and rolling pin to make sausages. But with these tasks, you would most certainly never match the efficiency of a mincer, meat slicer or sausage stuffer.

Meat mincer
In order to make successful salami, sausages or pâtés, you will require a meat mincer (also known as a grinder). This allows you to mince fairly large quantities of meat or offal into even, appropriately sized grains or morsels easily. You need to cut the meat into pieces small enough to fit into the top hole of the feeding plate, from where it is moved along the chamber by a spiralled 'worm'. The meat is then cut by a rotating blade before being forced through the end plate and into a bowl.

Pork minced on the coarse plate

Adding salami mix to a sausage stuffer

Most grinders come with three detachable blades and plates that dictate the texture of the minced meat. Each plate has several holes in it of uniform diameter, usually ranging from 10mm to 3mm, to give the meat either a coarse, medium or fine texture. I favour the coarse plate for sausages and salami; the medium one for burgers or processing scraps, off cuts and bits of 'trim'; and the finer plate for pâtés.

It is important to always match the right blade with the right plate because the blades are self-sharpening. If they're used with the wrong plate, they will eventually become blunt. A blunt blade will 'chew' meat and give it an unpleasant texture. Always tie the blade to the plate in a pair with butcher's string when it is not in use.

Apart from producing a lovely, clean-textured mince, the benefit of using a good meat grinder is that it will not transfer heat into its moving parts, so the temperature of the meat is not raised. To make sure none of the residual heat in the cleaned moving parts of the mincer transfers warmth to fresh meat during use, you should first cool the parts down in a deep tray of iced water, then dry and reassemble them ready for use.

You can mince meat in a food processor but it may transfer some heat to the meat and it will never give you the same evenly chopped texture as a proper grinder; the meat will be more of a coarse purée. I have had some success using a top-of-the-range domestic food processor, but I'd recommend you go for a good meat mincer. Superior models start at around £150; these are classed as domestic appliances. The model we use at River Cottage is designed for small- to medium-scale production and costs around £500.

Sausage filler

This allows you to force minced meat into a casing via a selection of nozzles. At the commercial end of the scale, there are automated sausage machines that fire out thousands of sausages in rapid succession from chambers that can hold hundreds of kilos of meat. However, all you need at home is a small, upright hand-cranked version with three nozzle attachments. You can pick up a reasonable one for around £100. As well as sausages, it can be used for salami, black pudding and a whole host of other recipes. This machine makes sausage-filling painless and stress-free without being overly mechanical – you're still very much hands-on, since you slide on the sausage skins and load in the meat.

By and large, the individual components of sausage fillers are the same. There is a chamber that holds the minced meat, which feeds down to the hole at the base, facing forwards from a protruding thread. Nozzles are attached to this thread and secured with a collar. Above the chamber there is a cylinder piston, which is wound down into the chamber by turning the handle, forcing the meat downwards. The piston must fit snugly into the chamber so that all the mix is forced down through the nozzle and into a skin.

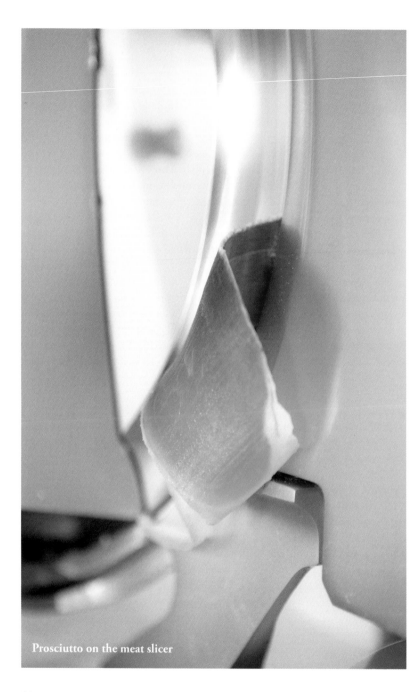

Prosciutto on the meat slicer

To ensure a cool operation, you should immerse the parts of the sausage stuffer in iced water before use (as for a meat mincer, see p.45). Most table-top sausage fillers have a clamp so they can be securely fixed to the work surface and won't move around when you apply pressure. I often think about inventing a musical version of a hand-cranked sausage filler but I'm not sure if there's a market for it.

Different nozzles work for different products. The largest one is used for haggis and large salami, such as mortadella. The medium nozzle works for most salami and large sausages, while the smaller one is reserved for thin sausages, such as chipolatas and pepperoni. The nozzle should be matched with the right casings (see p.86), which are fed on to it.

Meat slicer

This piece of kit will probably be the one you use the least, and it is expensive – expect to pay around £150 for a small domestic one, and up to £1,000 for something more heavy-duty. But when it comes to creating wafer-thin slices of ham, bacon, pastrami or bresaola, there is no substitute. The slicer plays no part in the making of the product but helps deliver it to the plate in its very best, most delicious form. It's the charcuterie equivalent of a stretch limo to the premiere. It can also tackle pieces of meat too hard to cut with even the sharpest knife.

The main consideration, other than cost and storage, is the range and size of products you will need to slice. If you will only be making a range of salami, for example, then you will only need a small, vertical flatbed slicer. A larger version of this model would also allow you to cut meats such as a boned ham or pastrami, as well as cured, boned pieces such as bacon and prosciutto. For a large piece of meat such as spalla or speck (see p.184), you would probably need to invest in a model with a supporting grip to hold the meat in place during operation.

A robust, gravity-fed slicer is the all-singing-all-dancing version that will have a large blade and the choice of belt or gear transmission. Belt transmission is functional and silent, whereas gear transmission allows you to calibrate the effort needed for the job in hand.

As with all equipment that has moving parts with the capacity to cut things, it is important to adhere to safe practice. Don't operate a meat slicer until you have read the instructions and fully understood how it works. Make sure the machine is standing on a flat, fixed surface and always have the protective guard or hopper in place. It's best, I think, to be ever so slightly scared every time you come to use a meat slicer. This will prevent you becoming cavalier and will make sure you totally focus on the job at hand.

These machines are substantial and not cheap but they can quickly turn a keen amateur into a seasoned professional. The improved results you get are significant. As with all machinery, cleanliness is vital (see p.54).

Knives and accessories

You could get by without some of the big machinery early on in your curing journey but you will need a small set of knives and a few accessories from the start. From basic preparation through curing and eventually air-drying, these items of kit are indispensable.

Knives

There is a vast array of knives on the market, which can seem bewildering, but you should only need a couple for curing and smoking at home. There is no need to spend a fortune on blades that have been forged and folded hundreds of times so that they are more akin to a samurai sword than a kitchen knife. You can buy good knives suited to a specific task for a reasonable price. I recommend a boning knife (curved or straight) and a chef's knife (sometimes referred to as a 'steak knife').

A boning knife designed for use with meat will have a thin blade with a small amount of flex and a sharp point, which is used to remove muscle from a joint. It will withstand constant contact with bone while allowing you to work in tight areas, such as the gap between a ball and socket joint in a pork shoulder, without damaging the meat. A boning knife for fish or poultry has much more flex in the blade and is not suitable for red meat.

A chef's or steak knife has a long blade and is mostly used for cutting up large pieces of meat – for instance, so they will fit into a mincer. These knives are also perfect for cutting slices and steaks from raw or cooked meat.

Steel

A steel will help you to keep a reasonably sharp knife sharp. It will not put an edge on a blunt knife; you would need a wet stone or professional knife sharpener to do that. A steel will extend the life of your blades. By passing a knife along the full length of the steel at an acute angle on both sides, you will keep an edge to it from tip to heel. I prefer to use a steel that is slightly oval in cross section, rather than completely round.

You should consider the condition of your knife before buying a steel. If the blade was sharp to begin with but has become dull, use a coarse-cut steel to get an edge back on it. If your knife is in good condition already, then a medium-cut steel will maintain it.

Butcher's saw

This piece of equipment will allow you to cut through bones quickly and efficiently. It is very similar to an ordinary hacksaw. The blade can be removed for cleaning and is replaceable when it loses its edge.

Butcher's saw and pork belly

Almost everyone I know has a hacksaw hanging in their shed or garage, and I understand the temptation to buy a new blade for it and just make do with that. I would advise against this; a new hacksaw won't cost you much, and it's far better to have one fit for the job. Keep the old one for tinkering with on DIY days.

Trays, boxes and brine bins

Food-standard trays are usually made from plastic and are designed to keep food in the best possible condition. Often they have embossed images of a crossed knife and fork to indicate that they are rated 'food standard'. They are extremely useful for curing meat in because they are hygienic and don't react with salt, unlike an aluminium bowl. They are very easy to come by, cheap and produced in many sizes. You will need a selection if you intend to dry-cure or brine any meat or fish.

You can, however, get by without these trays via a little clever redeployment of the salad drawers in your fridge. Empty these drawers, give them a thorough cleaning and put them back in place. Rename them 'curing boxes' and enjoy the eureka moment, knowing that those newly acquired bits of kit will allow you to cure everything from bacon to pastrami via bresaola, coppa and pancetta.

Food-standard trays and salad-drawer curing boxes can only hold small pieces of meat and at some point I hope you will want to create a significant, salted, air-dried chunk of cured meat such as a prosciutto ham from a fine pork leg (see recipe on p.156). In this case, you will need to invest in a couple of boxes, similar to the trays mentioned above but with much deeper sides, big enough to fit in a whole leg and a considerable amount of salt.

In the past I used to be a stickler for using wooden boxes – large wine boxes or pine boxes – but it was proven to me by my good friend Mark Diacono (writer, gardener, broadcaster) that plastic food-standard boxes actually work just as well, if not better. These boxes also double up as brine bins which can hold a significant amount of liquid and joints of meat.

Butcher's block

A butcher's block is not the unproductive procrastination process of someone in the meat trade with a looming deadline. It is an important work area where you will do most of your meat processing.

If you are only ever going to work with small pieces of meat, then an ordinary, sturdy wooden cutting board will probably suffice. But as soon as you graduate to larger pieces or whole carcasses, or if you expect to be butchering fairly often, it is really important to have a large, designated work surface.

There are variously sized professional blocks but even the smallest – at around 50cm square – are neither portable nor cheap. You have to view a butcher's block for what it is: a beautifully constructed permanent fixture – and an investment.

25kg NET

PREMIUM GRADE

pd...

PURE DRIED VACUUM SA...

FOOD GRADE PURITY

VACUUM SALT

INEOS
Enterprises

STORE IN A DRY PLACE

ANTI-CAKING AGENT (E55...

SHE... HALAAL CERTIFIED

PDV salt and large food-standard box

Prices start in the region of £700 and most blocks require a supporting aluminium stand too; you could even commission a bespoke block suited to your situation. The wood must be treated with oil and only cleaned with a wire brush, which takes the surface off like a planer. Water only serves to crack and ruin it.

I much prefer wooden boards to plastic ones. Wood has a better feel and also inherent anti-bacterial qualities. After a period of popularity for plastic blocks, the commercial sector is now favouring wood again too.

Butcher's string and hooks
These items are extremely useful for all charcuterie and salumi. Proper butcher's string allows you to tie joints as well as helping your salami to retain their shape. And stainless-steel hooks make hanging your produce easy and secure.

Jambon sac/muslin cloth
A jambon sac and a muslin cloth are used for the same purpose – to tie around meat to protect it while it is air-drying. A jambon sac is akin to a pillowcase – as the sac billows out, the air flows freely around the meat, helping to dry it out as well as allowing the natural yeasts and moulds in the air to colonise its surface. You can see through the cloth to monitor any changes in the meat's condition. A muslin cloth can be used but it is not as effective at letting air get to the meat.

Meat safe
A meat safe is essentially a box with sides made of fly mesh, held together by a wooden frame with one side hinged as a door, in which you can cure produce. You can easily construct one at home, or look for one at a car-boot sale or junk shop.

Measuring sundries

It is important to monitor the progress of your products throughout the curing process and also to make sure that the conditions you are keeping them in are favourable. The following instruments are a great reassurance.

Brinometer
Also known as a hydrometer or salinometer, this instrument will inform you how salty a brine is. A brinometer has a calibrated scale marked along its length. It sits vertically in the brine, resembling a glass fishing float, and the salinity is shown by how high the meter floats in the brine. It isn't an essential component of your tool kit – especially if you use measured quantities of salt and liquid – but it is a useful tool for checking simple brines (see pp.112–3).

Butcher's string

Butcher's hook

Muslin jambon sac

A brinometer

pH measure

This device allows you to measure the acidity of your curing produce, in order to ensure the correct level is maintained. It is particularly useful when making salami or fermented sausage, where the pH is crucial (see p.107). There are several ways to attain the correct pH but it is very reassuring to be able to accurately double-check it. Electronic pH readers have a probe, which you insert into the meat. You can also use pH strips but these are a little less precise.

Thermo-hygrometer

This will allow you to monitor the relative humidity – the relationship between water content and temperature in the air – in the place you designate for air-drying. A simple wall-mounted version will do the trick. You can alter the humidity by increasing the flow of air or by using a humidifier or dehumidifier. A bowl of heavily saturated salt water will also help raise humidity in the surrounding area if required.

At River Cottage we keep a record of temperatures, humidity and pH. This record is kept for the local Environmental Health Office but equally importantly it is a useful reference source for all the products that we cure. I am often pleasantly surprised by nuances of flavour or texture differences between products made to the same recipe, caused by variation in temperature, humidity or pH. By looking at the data I can attempt to replicate the process with the same conditions. I suggest you keep your own record, for reference for future products.

Cleaning your kit

Checking that your equipment is clean should be your first action before starting a recipe and cleaning your kit should be your last to ensure that you are operating within the best food safety, health and hygiene parameters. Every moving part from machines – blades, plates, knives, nozzles, handles and hoppers – should be scrupulously cleaned after use. Dismantle all moving parts of machines and either put through a dishwasher on a hot wash (above 65°C) or hand wash in a sink with a soap detergent, then allow to cool completely before reassembling. Don't put the plastic nozzles of your sausage stuffer in the dishwasher though, because they are liable to become brittle and break. Instead use a bottle brush to clean them after soaking in hot soapy water.

If you've got a butcher's block, do not soak it in water to clean it. Only use the recommended block brush which acts like a wood sander, stripping away the top surface of wood after every use.

Hanging salami before air-drying

Ingredients

Pork belly

Curing and smoking are not techniques to disguise inferior produce. They are ways to turn something good into an elevated version of itself. If you start with the best possible ingredients, you will get the best possible results. The trick is to use the methods to enhance an ingredient without losing its original flavours. They are adaptable techniques that can work their magic across almost anything – from meat and fish to cheese and vegetables.

Meat

In the following pages you will find tables that list various cuts of pork, beef, lamb and venison and the different curing techniques that work well on them. These are by no means exhaustive but offer a sound general overview that relates specifically to the recipes in this book.

First a word on buying your meat. At River Cottage we are lucky enough to be able to use whole carcasses – the majority of which are reared on our smallholding – and there is a definite economy of scale here. We can create many different cured products at a time because we can utilise every part of the carcass. Buying small, individual pieces is fine, especially when you are first experimenting with curing. But if you can buy half or a whole carcass – or even use your own animals – it will certainly work out to be better value in the long run.

Initially, buying a lot of meat in one go might seem daunting. But you don't have to use it all at once – in fact, it may be advantageous not to do so. It is one of life's peculiarities that meat which has been previously frozen cures exceptionally well (ironic, when you consider that curing came about in the first place because refrigeration was not available). Preserving meat is all about drawing out the moisture, which is exactly what happens when you allow frozen meat to thaw – water drains away and fibres open up. So buying in bulk and then freezing some of your meat is a great start to curing success.

Of all the types of meat you would possibly cure from a whole carcass or large cuts, pork is the most likely. It is so versatile and accessible. Of course, not everyone will be in the position to buy and use a whole carcass but this doesn't matter. The range of possibilities for turning pork into something cured is so extensive that even if you buy just one joint or cut of pork you have the option to turn it into several different things. It gives you choices and therefore it is an important ingredient in building your repertoire and furthering your knowledge.

As pork accounts for a large portion of the recipes in this book I thought it would be useful to include some basic butchery techniques (see pp.62–75), so that you can prepare joints of pork ready to turn into all of the products listed in the table on p.61.

Pork

The pig is the source of most of the well-known and celebrated cured goods. It is considered to be the original curing ingredient, particularly in the realms of charcuterie and salumi, although perhaps wild boar should really hold that title. Pork has a perfect ratio of fat to lean meat and it responds favourably to all sorts of curing techniques.

We are extremely good at producing pork in Britain, and have some of the highest welfare standards in the world. In terms of curing and smoking, it is only really bacon that is widely recognised as a typical British cured product. But that does not reflect the true potential of this meat, as you'll discover once you start dipping into the recipes.

You can learn everything you need to know about dry-curing, brines, moulds and smoking with a small, inexpensive piece of pork. A chump joint is the perfect practice piece – ideal to experiment with until your adventures in curing and smoking take you further afield.

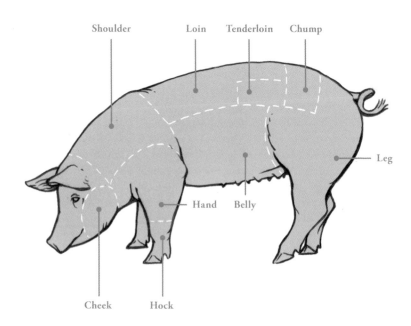

CUT	PRODUCT	TECHNIQUE	RECIPE
Hand	Salami	Fermentation, air-drying	p.167
	Chorizo	Fermentation, air-drying	p.171
	Cotechino	Fermentation, air-drying	p.175
	Hunter's sausage	Fermentation, cold-smoking	p.235
Shoulder	Spalla	Dry-curing	p.184
	Speck	Dry-curing, cold-smoking	p.184
	Salami	Fermentation, air-drying	p.167
	Coppa	Dry-curing	p.152
	Chorizo	Fermentation, air-drying	p.171
	Cotechino	Fermentation, air-drying	p.175
	Hunter's sausage	Fermentation, air-drying	p.235
Hock	Terrine	Wet-curing, air-drying, cold-smoking	p.239
Loin	Back bacon	Dry-curing	p.142
	Chorizo	Fermentation, air-drying	p.171
Belly	Streaky bacon	Dry-curing	p.138
	Pancetta	Dry-curing/brine hybrid, air-drying	p.145
Chump	Cured chump	Dry-curing	p.159
		Wet-curing, cold-smoking	p.195
Leg	Prosciutto	Total immersion method, air-drying	p.156
	Cider-cured ham	Wet-curing, air-drying, cold-smoking (optional)	p.195
Tenderloin	Filletto	Dry-curing, air-drying	p.178
	Hot-smoked	Dry-curing, hot-smoking	p.218
Back fat	Lardo	Dry-curing	p.151
Flare fat	Rendered	Confit (as for duck fat)	p.207

Skinning and boning a hand of pork

If you want to use the hock to make a terrine (see p.239), then saw it off the joint at this point.

To prepare the hand for mincing in order to make salami, chorizo, cotechino or hunter's sausage, place the joint on a cutting board or butcher's block skin side down and remove the small section of flat ribs from the underside of the hand and hock (pic 1). Keep these aside to use for stocks and sauces.

To remove the skin, turn the hock so that the end where the trotter was is now facing towards you with the skin uppermost. Insert the knife all the way in between the skin and the flesh and then rotate it through 90° so that the sharp edge is now pointing upwards underneath the skin. Keeping the fingers of your holding hand away from the knife, lift the knife so that it cuts through the skin all the way to the top of the joint (pic 2).

Remove the skin by running the blade underneath the skin and pulling it away carefully with your free hand (pic 3); it should come off in one sheet. The skin can be put on top of a soup or stew (it will partially render down and thicken it).

Starting at the knuckle end (pic 4), cut around the elbow joint to release it from the meat (pic 5), so that it can be pulled free (pic 6). The meat can now be cut into chunks, small enough to push through the mincer.

Boning a shoulder of pork

Place the shoulder skin side down on a cutting board or butcher's block so that you can clearly see the short row of top ribs and the spine extending into the neck bone. Slide the tip of the knife behind the top of the ribs and begin to separate the bone from the flesh using controlled strokes, keeping the knife close to the bones (pic 1). This will ensure you keep as much meat on the shoulder as possible. Follow the shape of the bone all the way down, using your other hand to prise the meat and bone apart (pic 2) until it is completely removed (pic 3). This bone can be kept for making a stock.

Locate the bone socket that protrudes from the meat. This is the blade bone. The blade bone can be quite tricky to remove because it has a flat side and a ridged side. With the shoulder joint still skin side down, the upper surface of the blade bone will be the flat side. Insert the knife just above the bone socket and cut along the flat bone to release the meat (pic 4), again using your free hand to gently prise open the meat (pic 5).

Trace around the outline of the bone and then run the knife underneath, keeping it as close to the bone as you can (pic 6). If you release the socket end of the bone first you can lift it enough so that you can see underneath the bone, paying particular attention to the raised ridge in the middle (pic 7). Navigate around the ridge as best you can and then remove the bone completely (pic 8). At this point the shoulder is ready to cure into spalla or speck.

If you wanted to mince the meat for salami, chorizo, cotechino or hunter's sausage you would remove the outer layer of skin (rind) at this point and cut the meat into small enough chunks to pass through the mincer.

To remove the eye of meat which is cured to make coppa (see p.152), turn the shoulder so that it is facing you sideways on with the 'head end' away from you. You should be able to easily identify a seam of connecting tissue just to the side of the large round eye of meat. Insert the knife and work it along this seam, rolling back the meat as you go (pics 9–11) until eventually it is removed (pic 12).

(continued overleaf)

Boning a shoulder of pork (continued)

Boning a loin of pork

Lay the pork loin skin side down on a board or butcher's block so the spine and ribs are visible. The long triangular bone attached to the top of the ribs at the spine end is the 'chine'. Saw horizontally under the length of the chine (pic 1) with a butcher's saw, taking care as you will be cutting towards your other hand. As it is released, hold the tail end of the bone out of the way (pic 2). Once the chine is removed, the other ends of the ribs are exposed and the loin is ready to make back bacon.

For Szechuan-cured pork loin on p.178, you will need to remove the bone from the eye of the meat. Insert the tip of the knife between the end of the ribs and the meat at one end (pic 3) and then follow the shape of the bone until your knife exits at the bottom end (pic 4). Then start to separate the top of the ribs from the meat along the length (pic 5). Keep the knife as close to the bone as possible (so as not to leave much meat on it) and use repeated strokes until the whole sheet of ribs and spine can be removed (pic 6). The ribs could be barbecued or used in a stock.

To make lardo you need to remove the fat from the meat in a nice thick slab (see recipe, p.151). The fat will probably have a visible seam, which you can use as a guide to cut along. This is best done when the loin is still chilled and the fat is firm.

Boning a belly of pork

To prepare the belly for streaky bacon you need to remove any flaps of meat on the flesh side and make the cut edges clean and straight (pic 1). This will make the surfaces relatively flat, which is beneficial for this method as you want the cure to act evenly. If there are flaps of meat or pockets of fat, the cure may not get underneath them and you will have areas that are not directly affected by the action of the cure mix.

If your piece of pork belly contains a section of rib bones, you can leave them in as the cure will penetrate through them. Only decide to remove them if you are proficient with the knife and feel confident that you can remove the bones in one sheet without leaving an undulating surface underneath where the bones sat. If you are left with peaks and troughs, as opposed to a flat surface, the cure mix will sit in the troughs and cause the cure to act in a less than uniform manner.

If you do decide to remove the rib bones from the belly, insert the knife at one end and work the blade relatively flat along the bones and as close as possible to them to cut the ribs free from the meat (pic 2).

There is no difference in the curing times if the bones are removed, or in fact if the piece of belly contained no bones in the first place.

More often than not, if the belly does have a section of rib bones there will also be an elongated strip of meat and connective tissue running along the bottom edge. This formed part of the diaphragm of the pig and creates a flap which should be removed. Simply cut it right back at the base along its length (pic 3) and remove. The meat from this flap can be retrieved, minced and used in any of the recipes originating from the shoulder or hand and hock joints.

As well as containing back fat there may also be a section of flare fat (see p.81) on the inside. Unless the flare fat is much thicker than the meat or is misshapen creating an uneven surface, you shouldn't need to remove it. If you do need to remove it then this is easily done by simply pulling it away from the flesh with your hand as if it were stuck on with Velcro.

Your prepared pork belly is now ready for curing (pic 4).

Preparing a belly of pork for pancetta

There are similarities between preparing pork belly for pancetta and the method for streaky bacon, but with the added requirement to remove the outer rind and rib bones for pancetta. The belly is left flat for streaky bacon but a traditional pancetta is boned and rolled after it has been cured so the removal of any bones is critical and the rind is removed so that the hard skin isn't tucked into the middle of the rolled pancetta (see pp.145–8).

The technique for adding the cure for both of these methods also differs and the preparation of the belly reflects this. With streaky bacon the cure isn't measured; instead it is applied liberally over 5 days and the liquid removed each day. With pancetta a measured amount of salt is added to the cure, which is in direct relation to the weight of the pork belly (once the rind and bones are removed) and it is applied only once. The liquid isn't removed but allowed to envelop the belly like a brine for a period of 3 days for every 500g of boneless, rindless belly.

To remove the rib bones for pancetta, place the belly rind side down and run the tip of the knife between the rib bones and the connecting flesh. Keep the knife relatively flat and against the bones to keep as much meat on the belly as possible. This way the surface of the meat should remain flat and even. Lift the sheet of bones up out of the way with your free hand (pic 1), like opening a book, until the bones are just connected at the base, which runs diagonally across the belly. It should now be easy to run the knife along the bottom of the bones to remove them.

If there are any large pieces of flare fat which create an uneven surface remove them. Sometimes the flare fat covers the whole underside of the belly, particularly if it is from the part of the belly towards the back leg. If it is fairly level there is no need to remove it.

Turn the belly over so that it is flat on a surface with the rind uppermost. Insert the knife just under the rind and score around the edges (pic 2). In a similar fashion to the removal of the rib bones, use your spare hand to pull back the rind (pic 3), so that you leave as much fat on the belly as you can. If possible, the rind should be thin and almost transparent. Once removed, it can be slashed and salted for crackling or used to thicken a soup or stew by placing it on the top.

Once the bones and rind have been removed the meat is ready to have the cure applied. If the piece of belly is quite big you may have to trim off one edge (pic 4) so that it will fit your vac or ziplock bag. Or get a bigger bag!

Boning a leg of pork

With all joints of meat being prepared for curing, you should remove any flaps of skin, meat or fat that will obstruct the cure mix penetrating evenly and successfully. This is also true of the leg. If there are any flaps, they will more often than not be around the exposed meat at the top of the leg and should be cut off so that the surface area is flat.

Traditionally the aitchbone is removed before curing a whole leg, whether it is a prosciutto, Ibérico or Parma ham. The first time you cure a whole leg you should leave this bone on because it is quite a tricky operation to remove it until you have improved your knife skills. Also, if you keep it on, then you are protecting the area around the femur bone underneath, which can cause a problem if it isn't salted well enough. The only adverse issue with leaving the aitchbone on is that it also acts as a barrier when you come to slice the ham once it is cured. So you do have to take it off eventually and although it is a bit tricky to do, it is more straightforward to remove it before the ham is cured because it is easier to get the knife around the bone when the meat is soft and fresh, as opposed to hard and rigid.

To remove the aitchbone, locate it and feel for the raised ridge running along it. Grab this ridge with your free hand – it will enable you to pull the bone away from the flesh once you have made some initial cuts, as well as keeping your free hand out of the way of the knife during this slightly tricky procedure. Remove any meat that is sitting on top of the aitchbone (pic 1) so that you can clearly see the shape and then trace the outline with the tip of the knife (pic 2).

Start to work the knife underneath the bone, which is fairly flat apart from the ridge that you hold until you can see the socket which has the 'ball' of the femur bone connected to it (pic 3). The ball and socket are connected by ligaments that you have to cut in order for the aitchbone to be removed. Get your knife in between the ball and socket and cut through the ligaments. Once this has been done you can work away at the rest of the meat so that you can eventually remove the whole aitchbone like a cap (pic 4).

Beef

Beef is much more associated with our food heritage than pork, though it isn't linked with traditional British curing techniques. This seems strange when you consider that we are all comfortable with the notion of well-hung, aged beef. But we have to look further afield for curing and smoking recipes that use beef. I think it makes sense to choose cuts of meat that we would traditionally use for a roast or slow-roast and apply a new European slant to them.

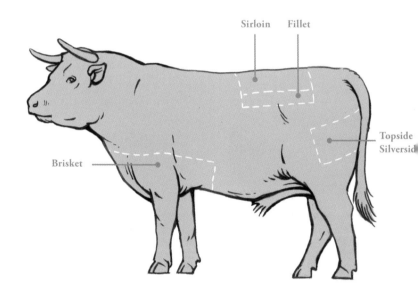

CUT	PRODUCT	TECHNIQUE	RECIPE
Silverside or topside	Bresaola	Dry-curing, wet-curing, air-drying	p.190
Brisket	Pastrami	Dry-curing/brine hybrid, air-drying, cold-smoking	p.233
	Salt beef	Wet-curing	p.200
Boned sirloin or fillet	Hot-smoked rose-cured beef	Dry-curing, hot-smoking	p.216

Lamb

I love the sweet tenderness of lamb but one of my pet hates is cold lamb fat, which is a bit of an obstacle when it comes to curing. The fat from lamb – tallow – was traditionally used in the making of candles and soap – perfect applications for it, in my opinion. There is also little or no fat marbling within lamb meat (unlike beef, say) so it can be a bit tricky to cure, and is something of an acquired taste. However, the recipes listed below work really well, particularly if you use meat from a hogget (a sheep in its second year).

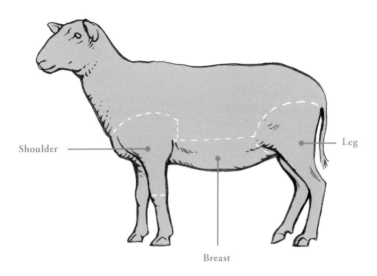

CUT	PRODUCT	TECHNIQUE	RECIPE
Leg	Culatello	Dry-curing/wet-curing hybrid, air-drying	p.192
	Oak-smoked spiced lamb	Marinade, barbecue hot-smoking	p.229
	Lamb violin	Dry-curing, air-drying	p.165
Shoulder	Pine-smoked Merguez	Cold-smoking	p.236
Breast	Lambcetta	Dry-curing, wet-curing, air-drying	p.147

Goat

Goat is very underrated as a meat but has wonderful gamey flavours when cured. It can be used to make exceptional salami when mixed with pork to up the fat ante, and the violin recipe illustrates a very traditional method of curing a leg.

CUT	PRODUCT	TECHNIQUE	RECIPE
Leg	Goat violin	Dry-curing	p.164

Game

As a lean meat, venison is perhaps not the obvious choice for curing but in fact there are various traditional recipes for it. In and around Scandinavia, elk and moose are used in salami – and of course standard biltong has springbok meat as its base, all of which share similar characteristics to venison.

CUT	PRODUCT	TECHNIQUE	RECIPE
Venison haunch	Biltong	Dry-curing, wet-curing, air-drying	p.188

Duck

Duck has a wonderful covering of fat and takes very well to curing. You can use either wild or farmed duck breasts to make a simple duck prosciutto by following the principles of a traditional dry-cured ham, or hot-smoke them using tea leaves and cedar plank.

CUT	PRODUCT	TECHNIQUE	RECIPE
Breast	Prosciutto	Dry-curing, air-drying	p.183
	Cedar-smoked	Dry-curing, hot-smoking	p.226
Leg	Confit	Dry-curing, confit	p.207

Fish

Both oily and white fish cure well and are perhaps more accessible and less daunting than large joints of meat. Fish was probably the first ingredient to be smoked and takes to this form of curing particularly well. I like to keep the flavour of the smoke quite subtle so that the taste of the fish isn't lost in the process. There are endless possibilities and I am yet to be disappointed with any fish I have smoked. Many wonderful dishes are created with smoked fish, such as kedgeree and chowder.

FISH	PRODUCT	TECHNIQUE	RECIPE
Salmon	Gravadlax	Dry-curing/brine hybrid	p.154
	Smoked fillets in prosciutto	Dry-curing, hot-smoking	p.225
Mackerel	Hot-smoked mackerel	Dry-curing, hot-smoking	p.212
Sea bream	Smoked fillets in prosciutto	Dry-curing, hot-smoking	p.225
Mussels	Pine-smoked mussels	Hot-smoking	p.220
Oysters	Hot-smoked oysters	Hot-smoking	p.223

Cheese and vegetables

It is simple and rewarding to smoke cheese and vegetables. There is little or no preparation needed – you simply put the ingredient in a cold (or sometimes hot) smoker and allow it to take on those exotic flavours over a few hours.

Oak-smoked Cheddar is a familiar product and this can be made at home (see p.243). Note that with thick-rinded cheeses, it is better to remove the rind so the smoke can fix itself to the surface. But you can cold-smoke soft cheeses such as Brie and Camembert too. I particularly love the flavour of a ripe, creamy Brie lightly smoked over beech or apple wood. You can also hot-smoke cheese (see p.227) by soaking a cedar plank in water and using it inside a kettle barbecue.

When it comes to smoking vegetables, the possibilities are endless. Garlic is more exotic once smoked, while cold-smoked potatoes take on an extra dimension in a summer salad (see p.244). Tomato passata can be hot-smoked, then spiked with cold-smoked chillies for a double whammy of smokiness.

You can also smoke your own herbs and spices – such as the paprika that gives chorizo its distinctive edge. The way to achieve all of these smoky herbs and spices is to lay a small piece of muslin cloth in the bottom of a colander or sieve and place the herb or spice on top of it in a cold smoker. The muslin cloth is fine enough to stop the ingredients from falling through but will allow the smoke to waft up through the colander and flavour the herbs and spices.

You could smoke your own black pepper and salt as well, which would add a smoky note to anything you cure even if you don't actually sit it in the cold smoker. Herbs and spices can be cold-smoked for several hours depending on how intense you want the finished flavour to be.

Rendering fat

Fat

In terms of curing and smoking, pork fat is the king. It is a rich source of flavour, it replaces some of the moisture lost in the drying process and it also acts as a protective barrier, allowing the curing process to take place over a longer period of time, which in turn helps flavour to develop further. There are several types of pork fat. You are unlikely to be able to buy any of these in a supermarket, but a good butcher will always prepare some for you.

Back fat This is the thick layer of firm fat found just below the rind running along the loin and around the shoulder. It's the fat that borders the meat in a rasher of back bacon. It is also removed and cured in sheets for the classic Italian speciality, lardo. Back fat can be used to fix flavour, texture and moistness in salami, black pudding, pâtés and terrines. It can also be wrapped around lean meats like venison to stop them drying out in the cooking process (a technique known as barding). As a commodity in the kitchen, back fat cannot be surpassed. It can be frozen and kept indefinitely.

Belly fat or flare fat This is an internal fat that lines the belly of a pig. It is softer than back fat and is present in streaky bacon. It is often found with striations of meat in it and is considered less pure than the back fat, but its meatiness can be used to advantage in some products. Belly fat is easy to remove from the belly and can be pulled off in sheets as if it were stuck on with Velcro. I sometimes add flare fat to sausages but I find the best use of it is to render it down to lard (as you would duck fat, see p.207) for confits.

Leaf lard fat During the slaughtering process, the lungs, liver, heart and spleen of the animal, collectively known as the 'pluck', are removed. These would spoil very quickly if left in place. The only organs left in the carcass are the kidneys because they are protected by leaf fat, also known as 'flead'. It is comparable to beef suet that surrounds ox kidneys. This fat is thick and brittle and is considered by many to be the best fat for making pastry, although in curing terms it would probably be used for rendering down in a confit.

Caul fat This membrane that lines the stomach and intestines of the pig looks like fine lace. It can be used to line terrines or as a replacement for sausage skins – or it can be wrapped around a lean joint such as a stuffed tenderloin, allowing the meat to keep its shape during the cooking process as well as browning and flavouring the surface. Caul fat should be soaked in water before use, to allow it to become as flexible as possible.

Salt

Salt comes in many varieties of differing quality. The two main methods by which salt is produced are mining from rocks and evaporation from sea water. Both methods have a long tradition. The latter is much older, although the Chinese began using wells to reach underground pools of salt water some 2,000 years ago.

Rock salt is simply crystallised salt, also known as halite. It is the result of the evaporation of ancient oceans that left large deposits, now deep underground. The process of getting rock salt to the table is more involved than that for sea salt. Rock salt is drilled out then put through several crushing and grading sequences before it is sorted into size and bagged. Or it may be mixed in deep wells with fresh water under high pressure and pumped to the surface as brine, and then evaporated at a refinery.

Sea salt is the remains of evaporated sea water, either allowed to form naturally, via the heat of the sun, in large shallow salt pans, or artificially heated to a point where the crystals form and can be harvested. If every sea and ocean in the world evaporated, there would be enough salt to cover the whole of North and South America 2.4km deep.

As rock salt is more extensively processed, it is often considered to be a lesser product than sea salt. Specifications for salt vary widely according to the intended use. Salt destined for human consumption must be much purer than salt used for, say, melting ice on a path or putting in your dishwasher.

For most purposes, salt can have a grey, pink, or brown tinge rather than being pure white. Fleur de Sel ('flower of salt') is regarded as one of the best-quality sea salts and this often has a greyish tint to it, stemming from residual sand particles in the pans where it is evaporated. There is also a microscopic alga *Dunalia salina*, commonly found in salt marshes, which can give salt a light-pink tint. This should not be confused with 'pink salt' which is salt pre-mixed with additional nitrates and nitrites.

The highest-graded salts have a more complex mineral make-up than ordinary table salt, containing various amounts of sodium chloride, calcium, magnesium, iodine, iron and potassium. Varying combinations of these contribute to the individual flavour of different salts. Certain minerals can cause problems – for example, calcium and magnesium both tend to make salt absorb more water, causing it to clump together or 'cake'. Often an anti-caking additive is mixed with the salt, such as sodium ferrocyanide 535, or a natural agent, such as magnesium carbonate, may be used.

At River Cottage the salt we use for curing is 'pure dried vacuum' (PDV) salt. Once the salt has been mined it is turned into PDV salt by evaporating a brine in a vacuum – a highly energy-efficient process because the brine boils at a lower temperature than the normal 100°C. As well as being 99.9% pure and affordable in large quantities, PDV salt granules are much finer than sea salt or rock salt. Under the microscope, they are cuboid in shape and all the grains are small and the same size. This means that they have an even effect on anything you are curing because the salt particles dissolve and penetrate at the same rate, giving a better overall cure. These small, even particles also lock together, creating a good covering for methods such as salt-box curing, which is used for large pieces of meat, like a leg of pork.

Sea salt is mostly formed of large crystals. They add fantastic flavour, texture and looks to a finished meal but dissolve unevenly and don't lock together. At River Cottage we mostly use this type of salt for seasoning or finishing off a dish rather than curing.

If you've followed other curing recipes, you will more than likely have come across different varieties of salt. In a lot of recipes originating in the US either kosher salt or pink salt is often used for curing. Kosher salt is a high-grade, large-crystal salt, usually free from any additives. The kosher tag refers to the fact that salt draws away any residual blood from the meat, in line with the rules for the preparation of kosher meat – the salt itself is not kosher. Pink salt is the collective term for synthetic curing mixes with added nitrites and nitrates such as Cures #1 and #2 (see pp.30–1), and Prague powder.

Salt should always be weighed not measured by volume because different salt crystals vary in their mass. Sea salt has a greater mass than PDV salt and so using the same volume of either would produce a different level of saltiness.

Sugars

Sugar is not an essential ingredient in curing but it does have its role. It can be added to both dry and wet cures and, as well as contributing sweetness, it has anti-microbial qualities similar to those of salt. I prefer sugars such as demerara or dark muscovado that retain some of their natural molasses, as this gives them a more robust flavour. Some demerara sugars are just refined white sugar that's been dyed brown again, so make sure you source a good-quality demerara.

You can also employ the sweetness of honey, maple syrup or black treacle in your cures, as is common in traditional bacon and baked ham recipes such as the cider-cured ham on p.195. But, on the whole, I prefer to stick with the brown sugars. They work really well with pork and beef, and in brines for poultry. The only exception is in the classic gravadlax cure (see p.154), where I prefer to use some caster sugar. Fish is much more delicate than meat and so a gentler sweetener is called for.

Herbs and spices for curing

Malt vinegar

I use malt vinegar to make the brine for biltong (p.188), and for wiping the outside of hams and salami that I intend to air-dry. It is a natural steriliser and raises the acidity level on the surface of the meat, helping to attract the desirable mould.

Always use good-quality malt vinegar as opposed to 'non-brewed condiment', which is the vinegar substitute you spray on fish and chips at the local chippy. This is a by-product of the oil industry and nowhere near the quality of malt vinegar.

Herbs and spices

There is no limit to the additional ingredients you could use to flavour your cures and this is an area where you can be really creative – but there are some traditional favourites that have stood the test of time for good reason, and it pays to be aware of these. For example, I wouldn't attempt to make chorizo without paprika, though I might add a slug of tequila instead of wine as a creative tweak.

I prefer to use fresh herbs because the flavours are more vibrant, but there is no shame in using dried herbs if that is all you have. I store fresh herbs like cut flowers, in a jug of water. If I need to keep them longer than a day I wrap the bunch in a clean paper towel and put it in the salad drawer of the fridge. Dried spices do not keep indefinitely as they lose their intensity. Keep them in sealed jars in a cool, dark cupboard and replace as necessary.

These are my favourite herbs and spices, with their key flavour characteristics:
- Black pepper Spicy and pungent
- White pepper Mild and musty
- Mace Delicate, fragrant and smooth
- Nutmeg As mace, but more bitter
- Garlic Pungent, spicy and sweet
- Paprika Sweet, aromatic, spicy and often smoky
- Coriander Sweet and floral
- Juniper Bitter and dry
- Sage Fragrant and piny
- Bay Strongly aromatic, with a hint of spice
- Thyme Fragrant and light
- Fennel Freshly pungent, with a hint of liquorice
- Cayenne Hot and spicy
- Tarragon Light anise flavour
- Clove Christmassy

Casings

You can use synthetic casings that are spun from collagen for your sausages and salami, but I prefer natural casings made from animal intestines. Synthetic casings often have an inferior texture and, although they are perhaps easier to buy, they are often more expensive because they are sold with a ready-made cure mix containing nitrates and nitrites (see pp.30–5).

Natural casings are put through a very stringent cleansing process before they are available for sale. They are stripped from the animal after slaughter, turned inside out, cleaned of their mucus membrane, turned back around and packed in salt. Different casings suit different products. Sheep's intestines are narrow and are used to make chipolata sausages. Pig's intestines (pork 'middles') are used for bangers, breakfast sausages or smaller salami, such as the hunter's sausage on p.235. Beef 'middles' and 'runners' are good for most salami and an ox 'bung' (which, when rehydrated, looks like one of Nora Batty's stockings) is used for cotechino and mortadella.

Natural casings should be rehydrated before use to maximise their elasticity. Do not hold them under a running tap because this will trap too much water in the skins, which will dilute the flavour of whatever you put in them. Instead you should just soak them in a bowl of cold water in advance of using them – a couple of hours should suffice. You can re-salt unused casings and store them in the fridge or freezer.

Natural casings do split on occasion but despite this slight annoyance I still prefer their superior texture. To me, biting into a sausage in a synthetic casing feels like eating something still in its wrapper. Natural casings, unsurprisingly, blend more into the product and don't feel like a barrier to the meat inside. And, of course, they have a more traditional look to them. You'll probably notice an unpleasant smell when you first open the packet but this soon disappears and doesn't carry through to the flavour of the meat you put in them. You can buy natural casings online (see Directory, p.248) or from your butcher.

Salted and rehydrated natural casings

Tied fresh salami

Filling and tying salami

Making salami is quite an operation and requires planning as well as preparation and some patience, but it is time well spent. The following method is the same for every salami you make, the only differences being the ingredients and length of maturing time.

I use natural casings for salami – normally beef runner casing, which is the lower intestine of a steer. These need to be pre-soaked in cold water for about 2 hours. You will also need to cut several pieces of string, each about 15cm in length, ready to tie the end of the casings.

Mince the meat coarsely, using the coarse (8–10mm) plate of your mincer, then mix it by hand with the correct ratios of salt and other ingredients, according to your chosen recipe.

Pack the mixture into the cleaned and cooled barrel of a sausage filler and place a medium nozzle on the end. Turn the handle so that any air trapped inside the barrel is released and you can see the salami mix filling the nozzle (pic 1, overleaf). Moisten the nozzle with a small amount of cold water. Open one end of a length of beef runner casing and feed it on to the nozzle (pic 2), leaving the end of the casing just hanging off the end (pic 3).

Tie the end of the casing with string, using a simple knot and leaving some string hanging down (pics 4 and 5).

Now twist the ends of the string into a new knot. When the knot is pulled tight, the string will form a loop (pics 6 and 7). The loop is important because it will make it easy to hang the salami for drying.

Push the casing back on to the nozzle. Fill the casing with the mixture to a length of 30cm or so, taking care not to overfill it (pic 8). Release any pockets of trapped air by pricking the skin with a sterilised pin or sausage pricker.

To secure the mix in the casing, tie a half-knot at the end of the sausage near the nozzle, using a second piece of string (pic 9). Pull a short length of runner off the nozzle.

Now tie a simple knot around the casing by the nozzle, using a third length of string. You will have a short length of empty casing in between two knotted pieces of string (pic 10). Cut the empty casing in the middle (pic 11). Finish off the knot on the second piece of string (pic 12), and create a loop as before.

Repeat the process with the remaining mixture.

Filling salami is something that you can easily do on your own but it is a simpler job when you have someone helping, sharing the tasks of filling, tying and hanging the finished salami.

Natural casings tend to bow into a horseshoe shape. I put the loops from both ends on one hook and hang them like this. However, if you hang them from one end only, they will straighten. It just depends on your aesthetic.

Filling and tying salami

Filling and tying salami (continued)

The salami should be hung initially in a warm place, at 25–27°C. This will enable incubation of the bacteria to take place and facilitate fermentation. After 12 hours in this environment, move the salami to your dry-curing spot, which should be between 10 and 18°C, with a humidity level ranging from 60–80% and a constant circulation of air. Make sure the salami are not touching a wall, or each other, and are not in direct sunlight.

Over the coming weeks, test the pH to ensure it is below 4.5. A white mould should form on the casings, indicating that this level has been reached.

The salami may take anything from 6–10 weeks to mature, depending on the conditions and the girth of the salami casing – the thicker the salami, the longer it takes to mature.

You can try the salami as soon as they are fairly firm to the touch and dry-looking, but they will continue to dry out and harden until they are practically rock hard. The exception is nduja salami (p.230), whose contents are eaten as a soft, spicy spread, taken from the salami at a much earlier stage.

When your salami reach the firmness you like, you can wipe off any mould from the outside with a cloth soaked in vinegar. This isn't essential but not everyone is comfortable with the appearance of mould.

Serve your salami cut into slices, 2–3mm thick. If you prefer, peel off the ring of casing from each slice before eating, although it is perfectly safe to eat.

The Methods

Over the past decade, through a very enjoyable process of trial and error, experimentation and success, I've learnt the simplest and most effective ways to cure and smoke fresh produce. Those tried and tested methods are outlined here in detail so that whichever of my recipes you choose to try, you'll have all the information you need to achieve great results. Curing and smoking will expand your culinary horizons – often literally, as large quantities, capacious containers and large bits of kit tend to be the order of the day – but, for the most part, the methods themselves are extremely simple.

Dry-curing

This is one of the most accessible forms of preservation: you are simply applying salt to a piece of fresh meat.

We have come a long way from the days when our ancestors sailed uncharted oceans to discover and claim for themselves 'new' lands, their ships groaning with preserved food. To create supplies for their journey, they simply packed fresh meat and fish in great vats of salt. It would have tasted pretty awful but it was edible.

These days, we no longer salt food out of necessity and our methods are much more refined. Knowledge and experience have taught us the minimum amount of salt required, and we've also learnt to include other ingredients that have a positive effect on the produce and also please the palate.

Curing should never be a way to mask the flavour of an inferior product, though all too often it is. Take bacon, for example: it is such a common commodity yet, despite its potential to turn a vegetarian into a carnivore at a single sniff, it is rarely as good as it should be. I am sure we have all experienced inferior bacon, perhaps bought from the corner shop on a Saturday morning, possibly under the influence of a slight hangover. It tends to have an oil-slick sheen to it and an inappropriately short use-by date for something purporting to be cured. On cooking, the rashers shrink to half their original size and leach out a grey-white precipitation. It also somehow retains the same colour it had on removing it from the packet.

This is not how it should be. What you are getting in that packet is a piece of pork that has been injected with a saline solution and some non-natural preservatives in order to keep it stable for the short period of time necessary to get it from factory to shop to plate.

At River Cottage we use a basic dry cure for our bacon. The mix consists of equal quantities of PDV salt and demerara sugar, to which we add finely chopped bay leaves (usually fresh, but dried is OK) and some cracked black pepper. I also like to add lightly bruised juniper berries (a favourite ingredient of mine) before mixing it all up. This simple cure delivers great results every time and is versatile

Basic cure mix

enough to work with many products; it is a launch pad to more elaborate cures and methods. Use it as a simple and delicious way into curing and then, as you get more confident and experienced, you can try other techniques and ingredients.

Salt is the common denominator in dry-curing but there are different ways of applying it. You can measure out the salt in proportion to the weight of meat you are curing, and leave the meat in contact with it for a set time. Alternatively, you can apply a smaller amount of fresh cure several times over a period of a week, tipping away the moisture drawn out of the meat on a daily basis.

You can also apply a dry cure once and allow it to turn into a brine without tipping the moisture away. Or, as in the case of a prosciutto or Parma-style ham, totally immerse a fine-quality leg of pork in a vast quantity of salt, remove it after a calculated period and leave it hanging for a year or until it has lost 30 per cent of its original weight.

Basic dry-cure method

The basic dry-cure technique works for both streaky and back bacon (although, because back bacon is a thicker piece of meat, it takes longer to execute). I consider this an entry-level method – not because it is inferior to other methods but because you don't have to be too precise with weights and percentages and yet the results are amazing, and will boost your confidence. This method also allows you to see the effects of curing almost immediately because, on applying the cure, moisture will visibly begin to leach out of the pork and, over the course of just a few days, the meat will become firmer and drier.

To make bacon, the cure mix is applied by hand to a piece of pork so that it has a liberal covering on all sides. It is then allowed to gently go about its business in a food-standard tray placed in a domestic fridge. Liquid will pool in the tray and you need to pour this away every day as well as applying another liberal handful of cure each day until the curing period has been completed (5 days for streaky, or 10 days for back bacon). Less and less liquid will pool out each day until the salt cure has reached equilibrium with the meat. The texture of the meat will become firmer and the colour darker – all tell-tale signs of the curing process in action. After the allotted curing time, you rinse off any residual cure from the meat and pat it dry with a clean tea towel. You then need to allow the bacon to mature and rest for the same number of days as you applied the cure to it, either back in your fridge or hanging in your designated air-drying spot (see p.103).

Salt-box method

This is a step on from the basic dry-curing method for bacon. The salt-box method is used when curing a whole muscle as in coppa (p.152), or with pork tenderloin to get it ready for hot-smoking (p.218). The weight of the meat can vary so it is

Base layer of cure mix

impossible to give a precise amount of cure in the recipe. Instead, you coat the surface of the meat uniformly with cure and leave it for a particular length of time, depending on the weight of the meat. A good rule of thumb is 1 day's curing for every kg of meat.

You need to place all your cure ingredients in a food-standard tray (or wooden salt box if you prefer), large enough to accommodate the meat while you are turning it in the cure. Make sure all the herbs and spices in your cure are evenly distributed through the salt. The cure ingredients don't need to be weighed but the meat does. Place the meat (or fish) in the cure and turn it so that the entire surface is covered. The amount that adheres naturally to the surface of the meat will be sufficient to cure it. Whole muscles or boneless joints are not susceptible to harmful bacteria or botulism, because bacteria cannot penetrate their interior. Air-drying will complete this curing process.

A minimum of 2% salt to the weight of meat gives consistent success, and 5% is the maximum salt you can use in a dry cure before the result starts to become unpalatable. Take into consideration that sea water on average has a 3.5% salinity level. I tend to adhere to a 3% salt ratio.

Total immersion method

This method is used to produce prosciutto or Parma-style ham. It is one of the oldest and simplest of techniques, usually applied to a whole back leg of pork, prior to a period of air-drying. You can apply the same technique to a chump joint, which is much smaller and therefore ready much sooner.

You need a lot of salt for this method because the meat must be completely buried in it. An average-sized leg of pork takes at least 25kg of PDV salt. That may sound excessive, but it is necessary. The golden rule for curing a ham in this way is to bury it in salt for 3 days per kg of meat. You should also apply a weight, such as another, unopened sack of salt, placed on a cutting board on top of the salted leg. This will help press moisture out of the buried ham. Unlike with other dry-curing, you won't need to empty the liquid out because it will be absorbed into the salt.

Obviously, you need a pretty big box for this method, ideally big enough to fit in a whole leg with the trotter still attached. In the past I have used boxes made from pine, or large wine boxes. I like the look and feel of wood. However, plastic boxes actually have an advantage over wood because they are slightly transparent and therefore it is easy to see if the salt isn't totally surrounding the leg inside. You can then adjust the position of the leg so that the salt runs into the gap. The other real advantage of using plastic boxes is that they are easy to clean and store.

Before you put your leg of pork in, you must weigh it so you can calculate the curing time, and also determine when it has lost 30% of its original weight and is therefore ready to eat raw. The full recipe for this method is on pp.156–9.

Total immersion method

Air-drying bresaola

Air-drying

With all dry-curing techniques, the application of the cure is only half the story. Once you have completed the salting stage, you still have to play the waiting game and allow the cure to mature the meat by air-drying. For some, this proves to be a psychological stumbling block because it can involve hanging meat not only outside of refrigeration but outside – literally.

It is perfectly possible to control or manipulate the conditions for air-drying cured meat without the need for expensive kit. The three main factors are humidity, temperature and flow of air. Creating the right environment could be as easy as finding a place out of direct sunlight, where the temperature is comfortable and a flow of air can move across the meat on a regular basis. Think porch or outbuilding, or a badly made shed or garage where the air can whistle through. Cellars can work as long as the air isn't stagnant – the meat must have a flow of air even if it means manufacturing it with a desk fan.

Of course, to minimise the risk of flies and to get the optimum humidity, temperature and airflow, it is only really advisable to hang curing meat outside at the right time of the year. In the UK, the perfect conditions usually occur between October and the end of April. You are looking for:

- Average temperatures between 10 and 18°C
- Average humidity between 60 and 80% (measured with a hygrometer)
- A constant flow of air

If you just can't reconcile yourself to the fact that your meat will be left to its own devices outside, there are several ways in which you can 'protect' it without negatively altering the process. You could use a jambon sac or muslin cloth wrapped loosely around it (see p.52); if the muslin is wrapped too tightly around the meat it will still allow flies to lay eggs through it. You could also manufacture a meat safe (see p.52) and I have known people to hang their hams in coarse fishing keep nets. As long as the mesh is small enough, your ham will not get fly eggs on it.

Even if you do get fly eggs on your ham or other cured meat, it isn't necessarily a problem. If you spot them in time (look for small, yellow-white clusters), you can easily just wipe them off with a cloth soaked in malt vinegar. A fly wants to lay eggs where it is wet and dark so they won't always be in the most open place. If the eggs get to the next stage of development then you have to confront maggots.

I have been curing hams like this for years and have only had two incidents with maggots. On the first occasion I was able to remove the small piece of the leg that contained the maggots and continued to air-dry the ham with great success. The second time, there was no rescuing the leg because the maggots had eaten through to the middle of it. The fly must have laid eggs on the ham even before it was packed in salt. Both hams were hung outside in early spring so perhaps, in retrospect, I was pushing it a bit, season-wise. Such pitfalls can happen to anyone but there are many things you can do to help prevent them.

If the idea of hanging meat outside in the right conditions still does not appeal to you, or if you want to cure meat all year round, you might need to invest in a bit of kit or at least commandeer a fridge for curing purposes only. You needn't spend a fortune on a second-hand fridge but you do need to use it only for curing and air-drying because it will be running at a higher temperature than a normal fridge, and any produce that you cure in there will ultimately attract mould. This will travel across to other products and although mould is ideal for curing, it isn't generally what you want on everything else in a normal fridge.

At River Cottage HQ, we have commercial curing fridges that enable us to control temperature and humidity. They also have large fans inside that turn air over the meat continuously. They are not very different to domestic fridges except that they are much bigger. However, as soon as the weather conditions permit, we hang our cured produce outside.

With a domestic fridge, you can set it to its warmest operating temperature for drying, around 10°C, though you wouldn't want to do this while there are other foods in it. Some modern fridges have different internal temperatures for different compartments, but they are not the norm.

Most fridges have an internal fan system as standard, so that air can circulate. If the humidity is very high, it will decrease slightly when the fan is on. If there is a freezer compartment, you need to make sure water does not drip from it on to your curing produce. On the warmest setting, the freezer unit doesn't freeze at all so water collects in the drip tray; this can spill over and needs to be cleared regularly.

If necessary, the humidity can be increased by leaving a bowl of heavily salted water (3:1 water to salt) on the bottom shelf. With the aid of a thermo-hygrometer (see p.54), mounted on the inside of the fridge, and the occasional testing of acidity with a pH meter, you can create home-cured products of the highest standard in a domestic fridge. You just won't be the talk of the village for having bits of meat hanging around the place.

Dry-curing ratios

Depending on the product, the ratio of salt to meat may or may not be critical.

- Whole muscles such as tenderloins and coppa are not reliant on precise curing ratios of salt to weight of meat. You could apply a 2% salt to weight of meat cure but I tend to make an approximate cure in a tray with all the relevant ingredients mixed in and then just coat the meat on all sides. This dredging effect ensures that the surface area of the whole muscle is covered, which will be sufficient to cure it successfully. The length of time the meat is left in the cure depends on what you intend to do with it. For example, a tenderloin would only need to be in the cure for an hour if you were going to hot-smoke it (see p.218). However, if you were intending to turn it into an air-dried filletto (see p.178) then you would need to leave it in the cure for a minimum of 1 day per kilo. This is also true of coppa.

- Pancetta requires a bit more thought because it is a dry cure that is applied once and allowed to turn into a brine. This cure is a precise 5% salt to weight of meat and the curing time is 3 days for every 500g. After the allotted time, pancetta is traditionally rolled, tied and air-dried although you could cook with it straight away. If you want to dry the pancetta and possibly eat it raw once it has lost around 30% of its original weight, it is important to make sure that the surface of the pancetta that becomes the internal rolled section has had sufficient contact with the cure because it will now be in a mostly anaerobic condition.

- Bacon can be cured without the need to weigh out any ingredients; it can all be done by eye. If you have roughly equal amounts of sugar and salt you will make a successful bacon cure. Additional ingredients such as bay leaves, cracked black pepper and juniper berries make a perfect cure. You don't even need to weigh the pork before adding the cure in approximate handfuls – it is all very relaxed. A belly of bacon will require 5 days of curing and 5 days' drying before it is ready to eat. Back bacon will require 10 days of each because it is thicker.

- Prosciutto-style hams are completely buried in salt for 3 days for every kg and air-dried.

When dry-cured items have lost 30% of their original weight they can be eaten raw.

Fermentation

While dry-curing is the action of salt on raw meat, fermentation is all about acidity. This form of curing most often refers to making salami. It involves deliberately keeping coarsely ground meat at warm room temperature for a specific amount of time in order to encourage the growth of certain bacteria. The meat is then stuffed into a casing and allowed to mature, unrefrigerated for all, or part, of its life.

Raw meat and warm temperatures are not usually a good combination because bacteria will begin to multiply, causing the meat to spoil. However, if you add salt to the meat first, at a carefully calculated percentage, it arrests the production of

Salami mix

harmful bacteria, promotes desirable bacteria and creates a natural acidity within the meat. The high acidity is key: you are looking for a pH of 4.9 or lower. You should check the acidity with a pH meter or strips (see p.54) within the first week and then at regular intervals over the next 6–8 weeks until it is ready. With the correct acidity, achieved by the right percentage of salt, white blooms will eventually appear on the outside of the salami to enhance and protect it. (I like to add a dash of red wine as well, to further raise acidity.) Fermentation also changes the texture of the meat, leaving it firm and full of flavour.

The minimum amount of salt required for fermentation is 2% of the weight of the meat. However, I often suggest a range of 2–3% because it is better to over-salt slightly, as the salt is critical for fermentation to work successfully. At 3%, the saltiness won't be overbearing.

At River Cottage, we usually fill our casings with our precisely salted meat mixture and then hang the salami in a warm environment overnight before moving them on to air-dry. However, you could put the meat mix in a warm environment overnight first, and then fill the casings afterwards. The advantage of this is that you can measure the pH before putting the mix in the skins and then use the mix as a salami starter – much like a sourdough starter for bread. I choose the former method because it involves handling the mix whilst it is still chilled and therefore working within a more controlled temperature range.

Backslopping

This rather unfortunately named technique (sometimes also called back batching) is a way of using a good fermented culture from a salami mixture to inoculate a fresh batch of meat. It's rather like making a sourdough bread starter and using it to get a batch of dough rising. This method is slightly more advanced than the tried and tested one above, and it is most often employed by professional artisan charcutiers and salumiers who are making salami on a continual basis.

The advantage of this method is that it pretty much ensures that the finished salami will be very close to the taste and texture of every other salami made by that producer because it will contain the same positive bacteria and flavours.

The process for backslopping is easy: mince your meat and add 2–3% salt to the weight of meat. Add all your other ingredients and mix thoroughly by hand so that they are evenly distributed through the meat. Place the meat in a food-standard tray or box, cover tightly with cling film and put in a warm environment, at around 25–27°C, to get the bacteria working and begin fermentation. You could also cover the box with a plastic bag for super safety, which will stop any light from turning the fat rancid. After a period of 12 hours or so in this warm place you can move the mixture to a fridge. Keep it in the fridge for 4 weeks without doing anything to it.

After 4 weeks remove the cling film and you will see that the surface of the meat has become discoloured and greyish, but underneath it's vibrant and pink. It should also begin to smell of salami. Transfer the fermented mixture to a clean bowl and re-mix it by hand so that the grey surface and pink underneath are combined.

You can use the fermented mixture to stuff into casings and make salami, which may slightly accelerate the process by a week or so. Set aside a small portion of the fermented mix and use it to kick-start your next batch by adding it into the fresh meat, thereby continuing with the process. The held-back fermented mix can be kept in the fridge for another 2 weeks before it is used to inoculate your next fresh salami mix.

If you are at all concerned about fermentation and yet still keen to make salami, then you should consider adding a commercial nitrate cure, i.e. cure #2 (see p.31) along with a bacteria starter. At River Cottage we use neither but are reliant on measuring the acidity with our pH meter and hanging in the correct conditions.

Wet-curing (brining)

Wet-curing usually involves immersing meat in a brine, which has a preservative effect. It also tenderises and enhances the flavour. However, you still have to cook anything that has been submerged in a brine, no matter how long it is left in there.

Brining has an elementary combination of water and salt as its basis. This saline solution can then be enhanced with herbs, spices, sweeteners and other seasonings to give it as much flavour as you require and, as long as you follow some simple rules on ratios of salt to liquid, you can be as creative as you like. Even the water can be partially replaced with other liquids such as beer, cider or apple juice.

At River Cottage, we make different strengths of brine for different products because they don't all respond to the brine in the same way. For example, we would not use the same strength of brine for a chicken breast as a pork shoulder.

Despite it sounding like the opposite of dry-curing, wet-curing has a similar effect on meat and fish. There is, though, an additional, seemingly contradictory action that takes place. Salt is a dehydrator and draws out moisture if applied in a dry cure. However, if you mix it with water, it has the effect of making meat more moist and juicy when cooked (Boxing Day gammon and Thanksgiving Day turkey are traditionally brined before cooking).

This moisture-enhancing effect is thought to be because salt acts on the protein structure of meat, causing the normally tight-fitting 'sheaths' around the muscle filaments to relax. Liquid from the brine is then deposited into the space that has been created and is retained even after cooking. This action also accounts for the fact that meat which is placed in brine will increase in weight by around 10%.

Pig's head in brine

Turkey in brine

Brines

It is perfectly acceptable just to use the same simple brine for all your curing (and I have included a basic all-purpose one here) but, should you start to feel more adventurous, I'd urge you to consider experimenting with brines that are specifically tailored for different produce. I have two separate brines for red meat and poultry (see overleaf), and all the recipes in this book adhere to their salinity and brining times – with further ingredients added for flavour.

Brines are easy to make. You simply measure out the liquid and salt, put them into a large stockpot and add all the other ingredients, then bring the brine up to boiling point, making sure you stir continuously so that the salt (and any sugar) dissolves. You then remove the pot from the heat and allow the brine to cool, before chilling it overnight in the fridge.

Do not add any meat, fish or poultry to a brine before it is completely cold or you will be creating a dangerous soup of partially cooked, raw and cured items. It is important that whatever you place in a brine is completely submerged. Putting a bowl on top to push down the meat usually works well.

Once the meat or fish is in the brine, chill it. The fridge is really the best place for this – although I have successfully left brining produce in a cold room before, and this may be necessary if you are curing a large piece that won't fit in the fridge.

Brine works more quickly than dry salt alone, and so brining times are shorter than dry-curing times. Precisely how long you need to leave the meat or poultry in the brine for depends on the size and thickness of the product you're curing and the strength of the brine. For reference, I have indicated generally accepted curing times for each of the basic brines overleaf. Obviously, the longer you leave something in a brine, the saltier it will become. Meat can reach a point where it has absorbed too much salt, which will then be released on cooking, so it's important to follow recipes closely and, when in doubt, err on the side of caution with brining times.

If you make too much brine, you can refrigerate the surplus until you're ready to use it. However, I recommend that you discard a brine once it has been used, since it will have been diluted and will contain impurities drawn out by the salt.

Measuring salinity

Wet-curing recipes always take into account the saltiness – or salinity – of the brine, which must be appropriate for the product being cured. You can generally just follow the recipe, but if you're interested (or if you have a strong flavour preference for the saltiness of your brines) then you can calculate the salinity before making the brine. I have included my recommended salt levels in the basic brines overleaf.

The easiest way to measure salinity is to use a brine tester, usually referred to as a brinometer, or hydrometer or salinometer (see p.52). Simply float the brinometer in the liquid and read off the number on the scale that is level with the surface of the liquid. A brinometer measures in 'salometer degrees', the highest being 100° and the lowest 0°. (This is not to be confused with the *percentage* of salt to liquid – the brinometer is in reality measuring liquid density, which is an indicator of salinity.

You can only use a brinometer if the brine just consists of liquid and dissolved salt. If there are other ingredients – such as joints of meat already curing – then the reading will tell you the density of the liquid rather than indicate how salty it is.)

Another way of measuring the saltiness of a cure you are making is to do a straightforward calculation: divide the weight of the salt by the combined weight of the salt and liquid, then multiply by 100. This will give you the overall percentage of salt to liquid. I have given salt-to-liquid percentages in the basic brines below.

If you want to create a brine from scratch using your own choice of ingredients, and you want to make sure that the salinity is appropriate, then a brine table may be useful. The table opposite gives the amounts of salt and liquid required for different strengths of brine. These quantities make about a litre of brine; you can increase them as needed. The table is very precise but you don't need to be too exact with measurements – if your brine is a little unsalty, it will just take longer to work. You will, of course, be cooking anything that has been wet-cured, so there is no health risk.

Basic all-purpose brine

For a simple brine, dissolve 300g salt in 454ml water. If you're interested, the strength of this brine can be worked out as: 300 ÷ (4.54 + 300) x 100 = 6.1% salt to liquid. This percentage is equivalent to 23° on the brinometer scale. (See above for a fuller explanation.)

In order to make up the right volume of brine, you will generally need about half the amount of brine to the weight of meat.

Brine for red meat and pork

The brine I use for meat is quite strong, 20% salt to liquid, which is equivalent to about 80° salinity. I often use it for shoulders or legs of pork, and I like to add dark brown sugar as well as cider and apple juice (see Cider-cured ham, p.195; Salt beef p.200; Brined Christmas turkey, p.205). At River Cottage, we wet-cure pork for 3 days per kg, and beef, lamb, venison or goat for no more than 1 day per kg. The longer time for pork reflects the amount of fat it carries.

Brine for poultry

This brine is subtler than the one used for meat. It has 10% salt to liquid, which is the equivalent to about 38° salinity. Poultry tends to dry out during cooking and this brine is particularly good at keeping the breast meat moist. It improves the flavour too.

A whole turkey can be cured for 48 hours while turkey breast is generally ready after 12 hours. A whole chicken or duck has an 8-hour cure in a wet brine but the breasts only require 2 hours. You could possibly exceed these times by an hour or two for a particularly moist and tender result, though of course the meat will taste saltier too.

Brining fish

In some parts of the world fish is brined. A highly salty brine is used because of the high percentage of water in fish and the brining time is short – just an hour or two. In reality I don't think it is worth brining fish so I haven't included a recipe.

BRINE TABLE

SALT (g)	LIQUID (ml)	PERCENTAGE OF SALT TO LIQUID (%)
26.8	990	2.64
37.9	986	3.7
49	983	4.75
60.3	979	5.81
71.9	976	6.86
83.6	972	7.92
95.4	968	8.97
107.5	964	10.03
119.6	960	11.09
132	955	12.14
144.5	951	13.2
157.2	946	14.25
170.1	941	15.31
183.2	936	16.37
196.5	932	17.42
210	926	18.48
223.5	921	19.53
237.4	916	20.59
251.5	911	21.64

Smoking

I have a fairly rudimentary approach to smoking. That is not to say that I hold it in anything other than the highest regard; I just prefer the simpler methods. You already know my views on kit so it will not surprise you to learn that both my hot and cold smokers are cobbled together from recycled bits and bobs. One thing that is worth bearing in mind, though, is that there will inevitably be smoke involved so you should make sure that there is good ventilation or an extraction fan in the place where you will be smoking.

Marked by a make-do-and-mend attitude inherited from my parents, I've made my hot smoker from an old enamel bread tin and my cold smoker is an empty cider barrel connected to a garden incinerator via a length of vent ducting. These contraptions are unique and full of character but, more importantly, they do the job really well. If you want to replicate something similar yourself, see pp.121–6.

Of course there are some amazing commercial, all-singing-all-dancing smokers. I have seen top-of-the-range versions that look like they could get you to Mars and back. You could also have a hybrid home-made/commercial smoker. Hugh has a commercial Maze firebox, which looks like a maze, in which he places wood chips or sawdust. It sits in the bottom of his smoking chamber formed from an old gun cabinet. This is tall enough to allow the smoke to cool before wafting over the products hanging in there. There is more control and precision with a commercial smoker but you'd be hard-pushed to say that they make things taste any better. And the principles are the same, whether you use a commercial smoker or not.

There are two distinct forms of smoking, hot and cold. Hot-smoking both flavours and cooks. It is hot because the source of the heat is close to the product being smoked. The temperature you would hope to reach during the process is between 50 and 90°C. Anything more than that tends to dry things out too much. On occasion, if you are hot-smoking and the internal temperature of the item you are smoking means it is not fully cooked, you might finish it off in a pan. I sometimes do this with large pork tenderloins.

Cold-smoking flavours and preserves but does not cook. The product being smoked is separated from the heat source so that the smoke is cool by the time it reaches it. The ideal maximum temperature for cold-smoking is 30°C. You will always need to cook cold-smoked meat, fish or poultry before eating it (with the exception of smoked salmon or trout).

Smoking cannot happen successfully unless the meat or fish has previously been cured with dry salt or in a brine. This is particularly important for any product that will be cold-smoked and not cooked thereafter. Even in the case of hot-smoking, a cure must be applied first. The exceptions are cheeses or vegetables, which needn't be salted first.

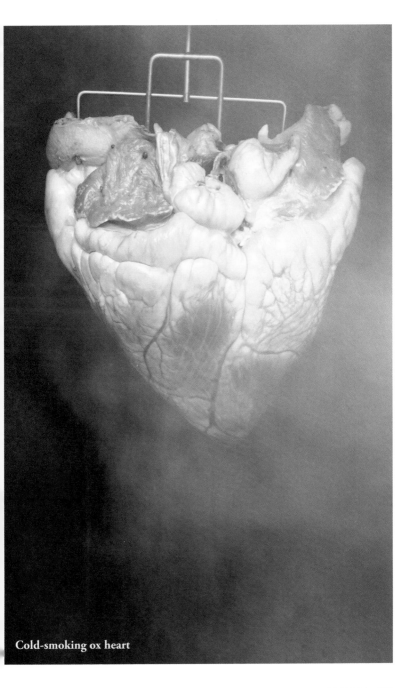

Cold-smoking ox heart

It's important that anything to be smoked is washed under cold water after being salted, to make sure any residual cure and impurities drawn from the meat are removed. But it's critical that the item is then dried again. It should be thoroughly blotted with a clean cotton cloth or kitchen paper. This creates a slightly sticky surface, called a pellicle, and that is where the smoky flavour resides. It is a misconception that smoke penetrates a product – it does not. All the smoky flavours are deposited on the outer surface. If you smoke a product that is still wet, the smoke particles will attach themselves to the residual moisture on the surface and create a brown, slightly smoky sludge, which then rubs off.

Cheese, garlic and certain vegetables don't form quite such a good pellicle as fish and meat. This means that though they are certainly worth smoking, you shouldn't expect them to develop the same depth of flavour as a side of bacon or a fillet of pollack. However, brined or lightly boiled vegetables that are allowed to cool and dry can take on a fairly intense smoky tang (see Smoked new potato salad, p.244).

Wood and smoke

I am obsessed with mixing woody cocktails from hardwood planks, chips, chunks, sawdust and papers to get the perfect smoky flavour. There are endless combinations which all have their own characteristic flavour spectrum.

Most wood-smoke flavours are created when lignin, a compound found in all trees, is ignited and forms phenolic chemicals. Softwoods such as pine also contain toxic resins which create harsh and acrid notes in smoke. This is why you should only use hardwoods, such as oak, beech or apple, for smoking food. You can, however, use pine needles for smoking, as these do not release harmful vapours.

Although you can create smoke from logs, twigs or chippings, I recommend using fine sawdust, small shavings or wood chips. These smaller pieces tend to burn evenly and consistently, giving a continuous flow of smoke, without forming flames. (If your fuel actually catches fire, you'll be topping up your firebox every 5 minutes, which is tedious, especially if you are cold-smoking a large bacon loin that could take up to 12 hours.)

There are exceptions to the sawdust rule. When I smoke on a barbecue, which is a less precise art, I sometimes go for larger pieces of wood. And, should you be lucky enough to have a large inglenook fireplace, you can smoke foods suspended in the chimney above smouldering logs.

You can also buy wood 'papers'. Designed for the barbecue, these are thin pieces of wood that you soak in water then wrap around the product you are smoking. To my mind, they don't really deliver on flavour.

Another barbecue smoking method is to make use of a plank, which is also soaked and then placed directly on the charcoal. It is suitable for small items like burgers, steaks, and chicken and duck breasts, and I have also used it successfully

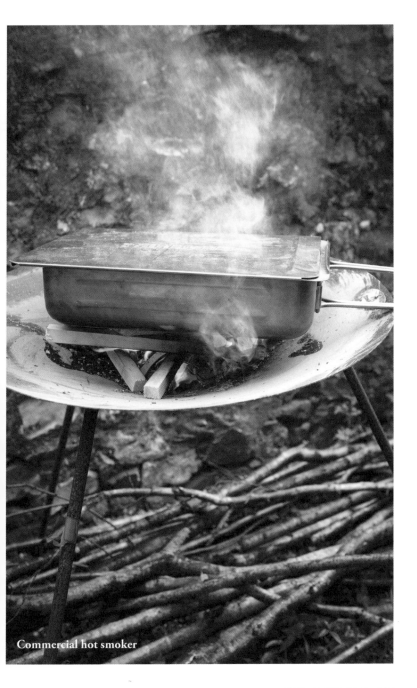

Commercial hot smoker

for cheese (see p.227). The smoky flavour is light but the method does work well. It's a good way to introduce some subtle smokiness into your food before embarking on the full-blown home-smoking methods.

In addition to wood, I have used hay, pine needles, bay, lavender, rosemary, nettles and juniper branches to create a more aromatic smoke at the end of a cold-smoking session, or for a blast of flavour during a quick hot-smoke of something to be finished off in a pan or barbecue. I also like to use tea leaves in some recipes, such as my Cedar-smoked duck breasts on p.226.

One of the great things about smoking is that somebody else's waste can be your fuel. At River Cottage we have a constant supply of clean hardwood chips and sawdust from the local sawmill and various craftsmen and carpenters. If you are able to get hold of your fuel from a similar source, just make sure it is clean. For example, anything that has been cut down using a chainsaw may harbour residual traces of chain oil that would create a toxic smoke.

And if you're not fortunate enough to have a local supply, you can use the internet to find wood chips and sawdust designed specifically for smoking.

I have set out in the table below an overview of wood types, smoke characteristics and foods they complement well. But don't be limited by my suggestions. Create your own combinations and match them to anything you please.

WOOD TYPE	SMOKY CHARACTERISTICS	GOOD PAIRED WITH
Alder	Mild and delicate	Fish and poultry
Apple	Mild and fruity	Hams, game birds and cheese
Cherry	Mild, sweet and fruity	Duck and venison
Beech and ash	Moderate and exotic	Pork, fish, poultry, lamb, cheese and vegetables
Oak	Strong, rich and pungent	Beef, pork, venison
Hickory	Strong, robust and bitter	Beef

Hot smokers

Portable hot smokers are available in all shapes and sizes, and many of them come with a little meths burner to place under the base and heat the sawdust to smouldering point. However, they are of variable quality, so take a good look around, and choose one that is robust and of simple design or, better still, make your own.

Mackerel fillets ready for hot-smoking

Home-made hot smoker

Building a hot smoker

Together with other members of the River Cottage team, including Hugh and head chef Gill Meller, I have built and used several hot and cold smokers, both at our first HQ and now at our permanent home at Park Farm. We continue with the same basic designs first and foremost because they work really well. They are also easy to make and, yes, they have a certain rustic character that seems fitting for River Cottage.

Making a hot smoker is *so* easy that frankly the term 'building' is a little flattering. It can take no more than 10 minutes, and may not require any more skill than scavenging a few bits from around the house. If you can lay your hands on a suitable tin – a deep one with a snug-fitting lid, such as a biscuit tin – improvise some kind of rack to fit inside it and locate a small pile of wood chips or sawdust, then all you need is a heat source to plonk the tin on and you're ready to hot-smoke.

Our own beloved hot smoker, formerly a bread bin, fits the bill admirably. This photograph was taken the first time we put it together and used it. That was a while ago, and we've used it dozens of times since, with great success. A little heavier and bigger than a biscuit tin, and with a lid that's easy to lift, it's still eminently portable and perfect for the job. We reckon it's still good for a few more years of heavy use.

To turn a bread bin into a hot smoker, all you need do is drill a couple of holes in each side, equally spaced and at the same height. Use an electric drill with a bit suitable for drilling metal. These holes can then support two close-fitting iron rods or metal barbecue skewers, which in turn support a rack. Make sure the length of the barbecue skewers or rods exceeds the width of the box by a few centimetres so they don't fall out. The rack needs to fit snugly inside. You can make a custom-sized rack from chicken wire.

A 1cm layer of wood chips or sawdust goes over the base of the smoker. This will be sufficient to smoke most things small enough to fit in this kind of smoker. The rack goes in with the food on it (always first lightly salted, rinsed and patted dry, see pp.114–16), then the lid goes on. The bin is then placed on the heat source – a gas burner, barbecue or the smouldering coals of a beach or riverside fire. The base of the tin heats up and the wood chips begins to smoulder, making smoke. The inside of the tin heats up, too – not to a very predictable temperature, given that the heat source varies, but with a bit of luck it will reach over 50°C and not exceed 90°C.

Depending on this temperature, and the thickness of the items being smoked, it may take anywhere between 15 minutes and an hour to complete the job and cook the food through. If the wood chips burn out before the food is cooked, you can add some more. To do this you will have to remove the rack and food – with suitably protected hands – and start again.

If you don't rate your own DIY skills, or your old enamel bread bin is too precious to let go, you can, of course, buy a portable hot smoker. If it can be used over various heat sources, such as fires and gas rings, so much the better. Of course, if you are going to hot-smoke over a gas hob in your kitchen, you should make sure that there is adequate ventilation – at best a good extraction hood.

Cold-smoking over an open fire

Before you launch into constructing a cold smoker, it's worth remembering that for centuries cold-smoking was achieved by simply hanging meat and fish above an open fire, indoors or out. And it can still be done like that if you have the right kind of fireplace. In the seventeenth-century farmhouse at River Cottage HQ, we have an ideal inglenook fireplace, large enough to walk into and stand upright. We've fixed a metal bar across the chimney at a height where we can just stretch up and hang hams, fish, salami and game. This is high enough that the smoke has time to cool before it reaches the food.

Ideally, for this sort of operation, you need low, smouldering embers. We would not hang anything in the chimney if the fire was hot enough to actually warm up the kitchen – the smoke would be too hot. Instead, we wait for the fire to die down and then hang produce overnight. If the fire is still a bit too lively, we dampen it with wood chips that have been soaked in water.

The best way to test the temperature in the smoking zone is with a digital thermometer. However, you can also hold your hand above the fire, exactly where the produce is going to hang. Ideally it should feel pleasantly warm (25–30°C). You can just about get away with uncomfortably warm (35–45°C) but any hotter than that and your meat or fish will get too dry – or even cook.

Building a cold smoker

If an existing fireplace is not an option, then the fulfilment of your cold-smoking ambitions may require the construction, or at least customisation, of a special bit of kit. A cold smoker is larger, more complex and definitely a bit more of a project than a hot smoker. Nevertheless, it's not difficult and you will be rewarded for your efforts with wonderful cold-smoked products.

Home-made cold smokers can take many forms but perhaps the simplest option is a version of the 'three-piece' cold smoker we now use at River Cottage. There are three basic components:

- A firebox to generate the smoke
- Some tubing, piping or ducting to move and cool the smoke
- A smoke chamber to hold the smoke and the food being smoked

A cold smoker can either be custom-built or adapted from salvaged items, so a good rummage around a car-boot sale or a junk shop is a wise first move.

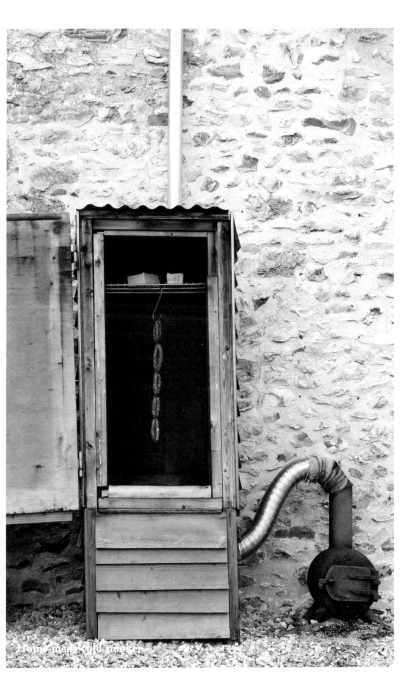

Home-made cold smoker

The firebox/smoke generator This is where the smoke is created, by burning wood chips or sawdust. At River Cottage we have a firebox made out of an old calor gas bottle. At home I use a galvanised metal garden incinerator. These are so good as fireboxes for cold smokers that they might as well have been designed specifically for that purpose. They are easy and cheap to buy, fare pretty well outside all year round, have neat, ready-made air holes to allow just enough oxygen flow to make wood chips smoulder, and conical lids that fit perfectly on to a piece of vent ducting. Also, because of the material they are made from, they have a nice, cool interior.

The only minor adjustment you have to make is to create a column of chicken-wire mesh to go inside the bin (about 15cm in diameter and around 60cm high), in which to place your fuel. A column of sawdust this high and wide will burn gently for 8–10 hours. To start the fire you just need to put a couple of hot coal embers or some lit newspaper on the top of the sawdust column.

Alternatively, you could dispense with the firebox and position a commercial smoke generator, just like the Maze version Hugh has, directly in the bottom of your smoke chamber – providing it is tall enough to allow the smoke to cool before it reaches the food above. This also takes away the need to incorporate tubing or piping.

The tubing/piping/ducting You'll need some kind of heatproof tubing that leads the smoke away from the firebox and over to the smoke chamber, allowing the smoke to cool as it does so. Spare bits of galvanised drainpipe (not plastic ones) will do the job, but are rigid and hard to work with. Flue ducting is an obvious and more practical alternative, as it's actually designed for the job of moving smoke from one place to another. It's also flexible, so it can be adapted to the space you're working in, and is cheap enough to be bought and cut to the length you require. It should be at least a metre long – more if your firebox has a tendency to burn hot – to allow the smoke to cool as it travels to the smoke chamber.

The smoke chamber This is the space where the cooled smoke is contained, making contact with the food as it swirls lazily around. A few leaky spots are ideal – if the chamber is totally airtight it won't draw properly. In some cases, a little chimney, or a least a small hole in the top of the chamber, may be necessary to help the draw. A colander placed where the tubing or piping enters the smoke chamber at the bottom will dissipate the smoke, stopping it from becoming too much of a plume.

Our first smoke chamber was an old cider barrel but the current one is made from recycled wood built into a large cabinet. The fish or meat is hung on loops of string from bars that run across the top of the wooden cabinet, though we can also insert racks, supported by some more bars across the middle of the cabinet, for smoking small fish or salami.

Other potential smoke chambers include old filing cabinets (the drawers can be adapted to hold racks and hanging bars), fridges, wooden wardrobes (beware of toxic paint, though), large metal dustbins, old tea chests or small sheds. You could even make a sturdy wooden box from scratch – anything from the size of a tea chest to a small walk-in wardrobe will work, depending on the extent of your ambition.

With any kind of smoke chamber, the ideal finishing touch is a temperature gauge set in the wall or door. Alternatively, you can measure the temperature from time to time using a probe thermometer, placed inside the chamber for 10 minutes while smoking. You should always try to keep the smoke chamber as cool as possible without letting the fire go out. Most of the time you should be in the desired 25–30°C zone but it can head north of 35°C in there on a very hot day, or when the firebox flares up a bit.

The temperature can be adjusted by altering the airflow through the smoker, which affects the intensity of the burn in the firebox. This can be done by covering or uncovering the air holes in the firebox, or by covering or uncovering the chimney on the smoke chamber. Either adjustment will make a difference of a few degrees.

Smoke-shack If you have the space and the inclination to do quite a bit of smoking, a small walk-in 'smoke-shack' might suit you very well. In some respects it is even simpler than the three-piece – being a one-piece, if you like. Effectively, it is a giant version of the hot smoker, in that sawdust is burned inside a sealed chamber, generating enough smoke to fill the whole space. Because of the sheer size of the chamber, the interior never gets too hot.

The classic customised smoke-shack is an old wooden shed. Bars and racks for hanging and laying food on can be arranged at about head height. A steel plate or solid roasting tin is propped up on bricks on the floor. That may sound like madness but provided you only ever light a small pile of sawdust in the centre of the floor space (and it must have a concrete or earth floor, not a wooden one) you'll be okay. Under the bricks, and under the tray, goes a single gas ring (attached by rubber tubing to a portable gas bottle kept outside the shack). A pile of sawdust goes in the tray. The gas ring is lit and kept very low. The pile of sawdust is lit, too; the door is closed and the smoking begins. The gas ring may be turned off once a good smoulder is under way, and the sawdust can be re-lit or topped up, as necessary. A small vent or chimney hole may be needed to keep the smoulder ticking over but, as often as not, a less than airtight door frame does the job on its own. If the shed isn't too big then you could also use a commercial Maze firebox to create smoke.

This arrangement can be adapted for all sorts of confined spaces, provided they are fireproof. Of course, you should never attempt to do any kind of cold-smoking inside a house unless you can take advantage of a large chimney space above an open fire.

Fire/smoke management Remember that the whole point of cold-smoking is to get the most possible smoke with the least possible heat – and fuel. In most cases, with the exception of open-fire smoking, a smouldering pile of sawdust is the best option. You'll need a few good handfuls of sawdust – more than you would use for hot-smoking. A pile the size of a 1kg bag of sugar should last 5 hours or more.

Lighting a pile of sawdust isn't always easy, and keeping it smouldering steadily can be tricky too. The first tip is to keep your sawdust scrupulously dry – store it in a sealed plastic bag or a dustbin with a lid on it. The second is that a blowtorch is an extremely useful item for getting reluctant sawdust to start burning. Aerating the sawdust and lighting it from within helps too, and a favoured item with many cold smokers is a short piece of steel pipe with holes drilled in it, inserted into the bottom of the pile of sawdust. Stick the flame of your blowtorch in that and you'll soon be well away. Chicken-wire column (see p.124) is just as effective.

In all cases, except smoking over an open fire (where logs are recommended), you should burn your sawdust, once it's lit, with restricted ventilation. This is essential if the sawdust is to smoulder, not flare up. But if you shut out the air entirely, the fire will soon extinguish itself. Successful management of a burn, and hence of a cold-smoking session, is therefore more often than not down to the control of ventilation.

Opening the door of the firebox a few millimetres (or the vent, if you have given it one) should increase the vigour of the burn. A small hole or little chimney in the top of the smoke chamber (if it doesn't leak already) will help draw the smoke through. Once the chamber is full of smoke, you can block it off – leaving perhaps just a tiny chink of a hole – with a smooth stone or block of wood. It's hard to be more specific than that, given that every home-built cold smoker will be different. But a decent bit of kit put together in line with the ideas above should be fairly forgiving. A tweak here and a tweak there will see you right.

Damp and humidity One of the factors that most affects the success of your cold-smoking is humidity – and this is obviously largely dependent on the weather. You need your smoke, and your smoke chamber, to be as dry as possible.

Commercial smokehouses recommend 20% humidity (not to be confused with the perfect air-drying humidity level of 60–80%). Commercial smokers often have some kind of dehumidifier built in to maintain conditions close to this level. Needless to say, at River Cottage we don't, and we don't worry much about it either.

Cold-smoking can be done pretty much all year round but I would not attempt it on blistering summer days – which will increase the internal temperature of the smoke chamber – or damp, foggy or rainy days, when the results are just not as good. There's no question that wetness is the enemy of a good smoke. For the same reason, any food you put in the smoker must itself be dry.

Cold-smoked streaky bacon

Barbecue smoking

Perhaps the gentlest way of beginning your smoking adventure is with a barbecue. A simple hot smoker, such as the one described on p.121, sits very happily directly on the embers of a standard family barbie, which is all you need to make the wood chips smoulder into life.

However, with a slight upgrade to a kettle barbecue – basically a round barbecue base with a domed lid – you can cook and smoke a whole range of produce, such as pork tenderloin, mussels, oysters, fish fillets, duck breasts and spiced butterflied leg of lamb (see pp.218–29).

Cooking with fire

There is no great mystery to cooking with fire – it is one of the most basic methods of creating something edible from a raw state. I think that primeval urge to make fire resonates with us all, however, there are a few simple rules that should be followed in order to move the results away from Palaeolithic towards culinary.

Forget trying to make do with a disposable version from the local garage – they are cheap, inefficient and probably toxic. The smoke generated from the cheapest versions will be black and sooty and this will be transferred to anything you cook on them. You have no control with this kind of barbecue and they burn quickly over a short period.

To get the best results when cooking and smoking with a barbecue, choose a charcoal-fired model, and one that has a lid. In order to successfully smoke as well as cook, it should have both top and bottom vents, which will allow you to control airflow and direct both smoke and heat. A kettle barbecue is relatively inexpensive and, with a small amount of effort – spent tending to the coals and wood chips to maintain temperature and smoke – should serve you well. (A foil pan or stainless-steel bowl filled with water, placed on the cooking rack next to the food, can further moderate temperature.)

If you would prefer something a bit more upmarket that requires less manual input to control temperature (and which can hold temperatures over a longer period, particularly in the lower temperature range) then you should probably opt for a water smoker.

Water smokers look like elongated kettle barbecues divided into three sections. The fuel section is on the bottom and contains a vent for airflow control. There is a middle section that holds a water pan which acts as a buffer between the heat of the fuel and the food on the grill above. The top section will have a lid with a thermometer and also contain a vent.

Because the heat reaches the food indirectly, the cooking is more in the form of convection or roasting than grilling. The separation of the food from the fuel by the water pan means the cooking temperature can be controlled easily and has a range between 80 and 240°C. This is particularly useful for cooking and smoking large items over a long period, such as a whole leg of lamb. Even though this form of cooking is at relatively low temperatures, it is still hot-smoking. Cold-smoking really needs to take place below 30°C and no barbecue, not even a water smoker, can achieve that.

I like to use pure hardwood charcoal for barbecuing – made from hardwood logs that have been heated to a high temperature in a low-oxygen environment. This stops the logs from burning too much but dries out all the sap and moisture, leaving a carbonised lump. This sort of charcoal is easy to light and burns evenly over a long time, producing gentle white smoke.

You can buy hardwood briquettes, which are compressed lumps of pure hardwood charcoal, but do not confuse these with standard barbecue briquettes, which are often made from coal and other materials such as clay and limestone held together with cornstarch and coated in lighter fluid that will flavour your food adversely. Make sure any charcoal you buy is from a sustainable source.

How to smoke on a charcoal grill

Most kettle barbecues have either a grate or a basket for the charcoal. If you want to hot-smoke anything for a period of 30 minutes or longer, position the charcoal so that it covers only one side of the grate. This leaves room on the other side to place a foil tray which can be filled with water if you want to try and lower the cooking temperature. There is no need to use water if you just want a quick cook and smoke. Instead of a foil water tray, you could dampen the wood chips briefly before applying.

Pile the charcoal so that it is two or three lumps deep and light it. If you are going to cook for longer than 30 minutes, you should place the foil tray of water in position, filled to the three-quarter mark. Open the bottom vents completely and place the cooking grill in position over the charcoal (and water). Some grills have hinges which allow you to add more charcoal and, equally importantly, wood, without having to dismantle the whole grill. Place the lid on top and completely open the top vent to create a good draw of air.

After 10 minutes the coals will be turning grey and the necessary temperature will be reached. At this point, add the wood chips to the burning charcoal and replace the lid.

When smoke starts to pour through the top vent, open the lid and place your food on the grill directly above the foil tray of water (if cooking for more than 30 minutes). Replace the lid. I like to position the top vent on the opposite side to the lit charcoal so that the smoke is drawn over the food before leaving via the vent. You can control the smokiness through the amount of wood added to the lit charcoal and also by closing the vent so that the smoke envelops the food for longer.

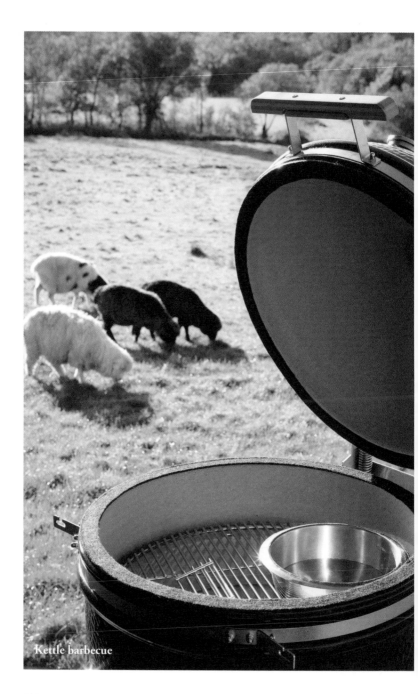
Kettle barbecue

How to smoke on a water smoker

With the middle and top sections of the barbecue removed, place a layer of charcoal on top of the grate, within the ring, and light it with the vents open. When the charcoal starts to develop a grey dusting of ash, place the middle section, with an empty water basin suspended in it, over the charcoal. The middle section has an access door so that you can add more coals or wood and this should be closed.

Fill the water pan three-quarters of the way up with water as soon as the middle section is in position. Put the cooking grills in place one on top of the other and put the lid on top. Leave the top vent completely open but adjust the bottom vent so that it is only half open. This will allow the barbecue to reach its ideal cooking range. When the thermometer is in the correct range (i.e. 90–110°C), you can open the access door and put the wood chips on the charcoal.

When the smoke pours through the top vent it is time to place the food on the cooking grills and replace the lid. The temperature might initially drop a little but should crawl back up after 10 minutes or so. You can further control the temperature by opening up the bottom vents to increase the heat and closing the top vent if the temperature is too high. The charcoal should easily burn for 4 hours in a water-smoker barbecue, although the water will need to be replaced every 2 hours. The water pan can also be accessed via the door in the middle section.

Barbecue rubs and marinades

Although I think it's important to treat your main ingredient with respect and never to mask or overpower it, barbecue cooking does provide ample opportunity to experiment with rubs and marinades, creating robust flavours and toothsome, sticky textures that enhance the meat or fish you are cooking.

Rubs

When you are smoking on a barbecue, you will need to apply salt to the item you are smoking too – not in the same quantities as if you were actually curing it, but enough to create the sticky pellicle (see p.116). This salt can often be part of a flavoursome rub.

Rubs are mostly a combination of ground spices, herbs and other aromatics and seasonings, including sugar and salt. They should be gently massaged all over the item that you intend to hot-smoke and allowed to flavour it for at least 30 minutes before cooking.

Rub flavourings can be divided roughly into six categories: hot, sweet, herby, earthy, sharp and salty. They can be used individually or in combination. There are no rules but, in my experience, hot and sweet work brilliantly together, and so do earthy and herby, while sharp flavours go well with anything on the barbecue. Try one of my suggestions or make up your own combination from the chart below.

Steak rub This is an excellent way to pep up steaks. Using a pestle and mortar, coarsely grind 2 tsp black peppercorns and 2 tsp mustard seeds with 2 tsp paprika, 1 tsp brown sugar and 1 tsp sea salt.

Hot and sweet rub This is ideal for red meat, pork and poultry. In a small bowl, mix 2 tbsp dark brown sugar with 2 tbsp ground cinnamon, 2 tsp dried thyme, 1 tsp grated nutmeg, ½ tsp ground allspice, ½ tsp ground mace and 2 tsp sea salt.

RUB FLAVOURINGS

HOT	SWEET	EARTHY	HERBY	SHARP
Black pepper	Allspice	Caraway	Basil	Garlic
Cayenne	Cinnamon	Cumin	Bay	Mustard
Chilli	Cloves	Paprika	Dill	Turmeric
	Nutmeg		Fennel	
	Honey		Marjoram	
	Maple syrup		Oregano	
	Sugar		Parsley	
			Rosemary	
			Sage	
			Thyme	

Marinades

These are a bit slower than rubs in their action. Often oil-based and supplemented with herbs, spices, fruit or chopped aromatics, such as garlic and onion, they allow flavour to permeate into the main product but they may also include an acidic ingredient such as vinegar or citrus juice which helps to tenderise it.

Spread the marinade all over the meat or fish and allow at least an hour for it to work, but overnight in the fridge is preferable to reach maximum flavour. Start off using one of my favourite marinades which follow, then experiment with different combinations of acid, oil and aromatics from the chart opposite.

Tikka marinade This is excellent for boneless lamb and poultry. In a small bowl, mix together 1 tsp salt, 2 tbsp garam masala, 2 tsp chilli powder, 2 tsp ground coriander, 2 tsp ground fenugreek, 2 tbsp freshly grated ginger, 4 finely chopped large garlic cloves, 2 tbsp natural yoghurt, a good squeeze of lime juice and 1–2 tbsp sunflower oil.

Citrus marinade This works particularly well with fish and poultry. In a small bowl, whisk together 4 tbsp extra virgin olive oil, 2 tbsp cider vinegar, 2 finely chopped garlic cloves, 4 tbsp chopped tarragon leaves, the finely grated zests and juice of 1 orange and 1 lemon, a good pinch of sea salt and ½ tsp black pepper.

Mustard marinade This works well with red meat, pork, poultry and seafood. In a small bowl, whisk together 3 tbsp mustard (of your choice), 3 tbsp extra virgin olive oil, 3 tbsp balsamic vinegar, a splash of Worcestershire sauce, 2 finely chopped garlic cloves, 1 tsp chopped thyme and a pinch of sea salt.

MARINADE FLAVOURINGS

ACID	OIL	AROMATICS	
Citrus juice	Olive	Black pepper	Oregano
Vinegars	Hemp	Garlic	Thyme
Wine	Rapeseed	Onion	Dill
Cider	Sesame	Ginger	Coriander seeds
Soy		Chilli	Paprika
		Rosemary	Allspice

Tips for successful barbecue smoking

Get the barbecue prepared in advance – and don't let the beer and wine flow too freely before you fire it up. Alcohol, fire, smoke and raw meat mingle happily, but can be disastrous if combined in the wrong quantity or order.

Make sure the barbecue is clean from the previous use – there is no reason to get sloppy about hygiene and food safety just because you are out of the kitchen. Invest in a good wire brush to clean the grills and make sure that soot and ash haven't blocked off any of the air vents.

Store your charcoal and wood chips in bins or containers so that they remain dry and safe (and free of any unwanted ingredients contributed by next door's cat).

Put your barbecue on a flat surface, away from anything that might catch fire, and don't leave it unattended – particularly if there are young children present. If you haven't invited the neighbours over then make sure they have not just hung out their washing.

Once the barbecue cooking and smoking is completed, shut the vents, replace the lid and allow the remaining fuels to slowly die down to ash at low temperatures. Don't try and quickly cool a lit barbecue by pouring water on it as this will just create a horrible sticky mess – and don't attempt to transport or move a barbecue that hasn't completely cooled down.

Recipes

These recipes are sound and tested but there is flexibility in most of them, as long as the core method is adhered to. The aim is not to have you knocking out identical products, as if from a template. You should allow for, and embrace, some positive contingency. Quite apart from the ingredients themselves, slight differences in humidity, temperature or the weather will lead to subtle changes in the end result. Using different cuts of meat may even result in products you prefer. Take it all as part of the on-going experience, and be happy in the knowledge that you are applying yourself to one of the oldest culinary frontiers.

The recipes are roughly arranged according to the method of curing involved, starting with the simplest techniques and progressing to more advanced methods. Although there are some recipes where the main ingredients are set (you wouldn't veer away from beef, for instance, if you wanted to make classic pastrami), I hope you will try all sorts of variations – I have included suggestions along the way.

Cured products such as confits, pâtés, hams, bacon and salami rely on slightly different techniques but they are connected by the use of salt and fat and most, while requiring very few ingredients, become much more than the sum of their parts. Confits are usually cooked in fat, which seals and preserves the meat when the fat is cooled and hardened. Pâtés are also cooked but have a nice balance of fat and salt to give them a moist texture. Often at River Cottage we line the pâté mould or tin with bacon and use off-cuts of cured bacon to add flavour.

Hams can be dry-salted or immersed in a brine – either to be air-dried over many months then eaten raw or to be cooked in a pot like a Christmas gammon. They take in a whole gamut of techniques, including dry-curing, brining and sweetening with sugar, syrup or honey. Ham can be rolled like a pancetta with spices, then added to soups, stews or pasta sauces, or simply sliced and eaten raw after cold-smoking. Salami require casings and a specific fat and salt ratio which allows a fermentation to happen. This method requires precision and some skill but is absolutely accessible to anyone willing to try.

Of course you should cook the recipes that most appeal to you, but there is one joint of meat I recommend you make part of your shopping list: the pork chump. This is inexpensive and incredibly versatile: it can be dry-cured, brined, hot- and cold-smoked. You can learn everything there is to know about curing, smoking, drying, moulds and bacteria by applying all the traditional methods to it. What's more, the relatively small size of a normal chump joint means it can be ready to eat in a short time. A dry-cured chump, salted in the style of a prosciutto ham, is ready within 4 months as opposed to at least 12 months for the traditional whole leg. Similarly, a brined and cold-smoked chump, cooked in the same way as a cider-cured ham, takes days instead of weeks to make it to the dinner table. There is no place for impatience in smoking and curing – we are not dealing with fast food here – but a chump joint takes the steepness out of a wonderful learning curve.

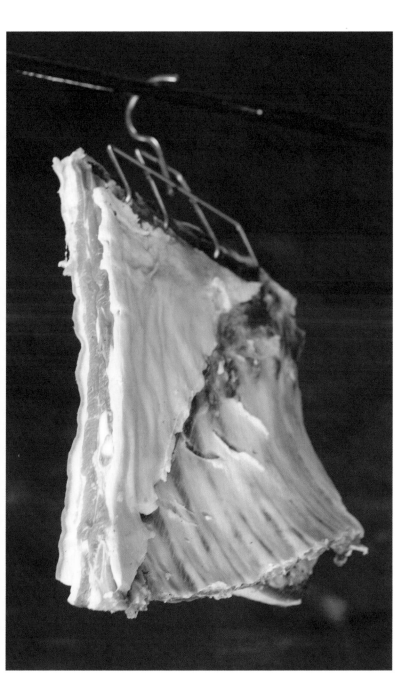

Dry-cured streaky bacon

TECHNIQUES	Dry-curing, air-drying, cold-smoking (optional)
CURING TIME	Minimum 10 days

The daily application of a simple cure, consisting of sugar, salt and a few aromatics, to a small, inexpensive piece of pork belly creates perfect bacon in just 10 days. You will learn almost everything you need to know about curing and hanging a piece of meat from this straightforward recipe, which is illustrated with step-by-step photographs on pp.140–1. It is simple but effective: the charcuterie equivalent of a haiku.

Makes about 100 medium rashers

2kg free-range pork belly, in one piece,
    skin on, flat rib bones intact

For the cure
500g PDV salt
500g demerara sugar
A few bay leaves, shredded
About 20 juniper berries, lightly bruised
25g black peppercorns, freshly ground

Equipment
Food-standard bowl
Food-standard box or tray
Meat slicer (optional)

If your pork belly carries an even covering of flare fat, keep it in place. An uneven covering of flare fat could affect the curing time so it is better to remove it and render it down to make lard. The fat is easy to remove: just pull it away by hand. It will keep in the freezer for months.

Place all the cure ingredients in a clean food-standard container. A rounded bowl is ideal because it enables you to thoroughly mix the ingredients with no pockets of salt, sugar or flavourings caught in any corners.

Place a handful of this cure in the base of a food-standard box or tray, big enough to hold the piece of belly. You might find the salad box in the bottom of your fridge is perfect for this. Add the piece of belly, skin side down, and scatter another handful of cure over the surface (pic 1, overleaf). You should use about a fifth of the cure on this first day. Lightly rub the cure into the meat, making sure that the sides are also coated (pic 2). You do not need to massage the cure hard into the pork belly but make sure it is evenly coated (pic 3).

Slide the salad box back into the fridge or, if you are using a separate container, cover it with a clean tea towel and put it in the fridge or a cool place such as a larder. Leave for 24 hours. In the meantime, store the cure in an airtight plastic box so it doesn't absorb moisture from the air and become damp.

The next day, there will be a pool of liquid in the container with the pork belly – a mixture of moisture drawn out from the meat and dissolved cure (pic 4). This is the curing process in action. Lift out the belly (pic 5) and pour off this liquid. There is no further culinary use for it. There is no need to be too fastidious and it is fine for there to be some residual traces of dissolved cure left in the box.

Now put a fresh handful of the cure into the container and place the pork belly back, on top. You can rotate the belly in order to even out the application of cure mix but this isn't strictly necessary. As before, rub the belly with more cure mix – again, aim to use about a fifth of what you started with.

Repeat this process for up to 5 days. You will notice that the belly will get firmer and darker in colour and there will be less liquid to pour away each day as the meat cures and dries.

After 5 days of applying cure, take the belly out of the container and run it under cold water. Then clean the surface of the meat with a cloth soaked in malt vinegar and pat dry (pic 6).

At this point, you can pop your meat back in the container (cleaning it out first) in the fridge or pantry. Alternatively, assuming it's the right time of year, you can hang the meat outside (see p.103). Insert hooks along one end of the belly or skewer it on to a rack of hooks, often called a 'bacon comb' (pic 7). Find a spot out of direct sunlight where the air can get to the meat and hang the meat there (pic 8) for 5 days. If you like you can wrap the belly in muslin, but this is not necessary.

You do not have to do anything to it during this period – however, you might want to give it a cursory check every now and then, particularly if you are hanging it outside. In the winter months you will not have to worry about flies laying eggs on the meat but it is good practice to check it regularly to see if the sun is on it at certain times of the day, or to see if there is a breeze blowing over it.

After 5 days it will be ready to slice with a sharp knife or meat slicer and eat. It will be the best bacon you have ever had.

You can keep the bacon hanging in a cool place, or store it in the fridge, for up to 3 months. It will become firmer the longer you leave it and the flavour will intensify. Cut slices as you need them, removing the bones as you come to them. Sliced rashers can be kept in the freezer.

Curing and hanging pork belly

After 4–5 months of drying, the belly will become so firm that it will no longer be possible to slice it but you can take chunks from it to add to soups, stews or pasta sauces. Eventually, it will become very hard and you will only be able to carve shards from it – these can be eaten raw. However, it is unlikely that you will have the willpower to allow it to get to this stage!

If you want to smoke your bacon, allow it to dry for 10–14 days before you do so. This will ensure that it is fully cured and will not be susceptible to negative bacteria, which are sometimes present in a smoking environment. You can then place it in your cold smoker and smoke it for 8–10 hours.

Variation

Back bacon If you want to make your own back bacon, use a loin of pork. As this meat is thicker, you will need to apply the cure for 10 days and follow with 10 days' hanging/resting.

As with the belly, it is better to keep the loin on the bone. If you remove the bones at this stage you will be left with 'peaks and troughs' in the meat where the cure can collect and act unevenly.

There is a significant part of the spine in the loin, called the chine, which needs to be removed because it acts as a barrier to the cure. It extends the whole length of the loin and looks triangular in shape. To remove it, you need to use a butcher's saw and cut along the spine at an angle, so as not to cut into the meat underneath the bone. It's quite a tricky operation but perfectly possible to do yourself (see p.68). Alternatively, your butcher should be happy to do it for you. The main issue is that the saw needs to cut horizontally, and towards your other hand. With care, the chine bone will come away, leaving a line of exposed rib ends underneath. These are often called buttons because of their circularity.

Once the initial drying time of 10 days has passed and you want to take a few slices off your cured bacon, remove the bones as necessary. A quick and effective way of removing them is to get a looped piece of butcher's string, or even a cheese wire, around the 'button' part of the ribs and then pull down along the bone. With a bit of effort, the rib will come away from the bacon, stripped of all the meat and sitting proud. It is then a simple operation to release it at the other end. These bones can be added to stocks to deepen the flavour.

Rolled pancetta

TECHNIQUES	Dry-curing/brine hybrid, air-drying
CURING TIME	Minimum 12 days

Traditionally, a pancetta is a boned and rolled cured piece of pork belly which, depending on its age, is either cooked and used for dishes such as spaghetti carbonara, or eaten raw.

This is really a more advanced version of the streaky bacon (on pp.138–42). The difference here is that the skin and bones are removed and the meat is rolled and tied. Also, with pancetta, the liquid is not removed as the belly cures but allowed to create a brine which envelops the belly. In essence, you are making a dry cure that turns into a wet cure.

The cure itself requires precise measurements, because you make only one application, and the time needed for the curing is linked intrinsically to the weight of the pork belly. The golden rules are that the salt in your cure mix should be 5% of the starting trimmed, skinned and boned weight of the pork belly – so 100g salt for a 2kg piece of belly – and to allow 3 days of curing for each 500g.

For ease, the recipe assumes you're using a normal-sized cut but if you are using a different-sized piece of meat, you should calculate the salt accordingly.

Makes about 100 round rashers

2kg free-range pork belly, in one piece
1 garlic clove, peeled and crushed
  (optional)

For the cure

100g PDV salt
40g black peppercorns, coarsely ground
50g soft dark brown sugar
10g juniper berries, crushed
4g coarsely grated nutmeg
4 sprigs of thyme
4 bay leaves, shredded

Equipment

Vac-pack or ziplock food bag
Vac-pack machine (optional)
Butcher's string
Food-standard tray
Meat slicer (optional)

Using a sharp meat filleting knife, remove all the flat ribs from the belly (see p.70); save for adding to stocks. It is also best to remove any flare fat (see p.81), which you can freeze or render down for roast potatoes, as for duck fat (see p.207).

Remove the uppermost part of the skin from the fat, by cutting just under the rind and stroking the tip of the knife underneath until you can begin to peel it back in one piece. This skin has several uses, such as placing on top of a stew, which it will thicken, or barding (wrapping around) lean meat, such as venison or rabbit, to prevent it drying during cooking. Trim the belly to make a neat square and, as ever, don't waste the trimmings – keep them for pasta sauces, soups and stews.

Keeping back half of the black pepper, mix the ingredients for the cure together in a bowl. Put half the cure in a vac-pack or ziplock food bag. Put the pork belly in the bag, laying it on top of the cure and then spread the remaining cure on the uncovered side of the pork belly so that it is sandwiched between the cure.

Seal the bag and place in a shallow food-standard tray in the fridge. Allow 3 days of curing for each 500g meat. Without removing it from the bag, massage the cure into the belly every now and again to redistribute all the ingredients evenly.

After the allotted curing time, remove the belly from the bag, wash off any residual cure under cold running water and pat the meat dry with a clean tea towel. Lay the belly fat side down on a board and rub crushed garlic all over the inside of the meat, if you like. Sprinkle the reserved pepper on to the area just rubbed with garlic.

Position the pork belly so that the natural top part is away from you, and roll the bottom towards it; these will almost certainly be the two longest sides. Roll as tightly as you can. To keep it in place until you tie the first knot, you can use skewers. Your meat is now ready to tie, using the butcher's knot (see pp.148–9).

Once the pancetta is rolled and tied, it is ready to hang in a cool, humid place (see p.103) out of direct sunlight – or you can place it on a tray in the fridge. The humidity stops the pancetta drying out too quickly.

Traditionally, pancetta was created to cook with and not necessarily allowed to dry out completely. However, if nice and dry, it certainly works well on a charcuterie plate. You can start to cook with your pancetta straight away, although you are slightly cheating yourself because it will have much more flavour if left to hang for 2–3 weeks.

The pancetta will be mature enough to eat raw after 4–6 weeks or, as a general rule of thumb, once it has lost around 30% of its original weight. It will last a couple of months or longer in the fridge. Either slice with a sharp knife or meat slicer.

Variation

Lambcetta This works as well as pancetta in pasta sauces. Replace the pork belly with lamb's breast, another inexpensive cut. I always cook lambcetta (as I call it) rather than eat it raw because I find lamb fat more palatable this way.

Tying the butcher's knot

Always start with your first knot in the middle and then one at each end (this will stop the rolled joint splaying out). Add knots in between at 5cm or so intervals. For pancetta, the strings need to be super-tight to ensure there are no pockets of air and to account for any shrinkage as the meat dries. For boned and rolled meat to be cooked, the string needn't be tight – it simply needs to keep the joint in shape.

To tie the butcher's knot, make a small knot at the end of the length of butcher's string (pic 1). Place the string underneath the rolled pancetta with the small knot pointing away from you in the '12 o'clock position'. Pick up the knotted end and pass it over the pancetta and under and around the back of the tail part of string (pic 2); you will need to pass it from one hand to the other.

Loop the knotted end over the top of the string sitting on the pancetta and pass the knot under and then up through that loop (pic 3), then pull until it forms a second knot below the original small knot. Let go of the small knotted end.

Pick up the long tail and pull this upwards (pic 4) and towards you so that the two knots are forced together, causing the string around the pancetta to shorten and tighten (pic 5). Pull as hard as you can so that the string will not become baggy as the meat dries out and reduces in size. Cut the string close to the knots (pic 6).

3

4

5

6

Lardo

TECHNIQUE	Dry-curing
CURING TIME	Minimum 3 months

Lardo is pure cured pork back fat, a simple but exquisite food. The world's most famous lardo has been made in the hamlet of Colonatta, in northern Italy, for centuries. Here, in ancient quarries, beautiful blue-white carrera marble is mined, a stone of such quality that it has been the choice of architects and artists through the ages. Michelangelo's David was carved from it. The same highly prized marble is used to make casks in which lardo is cured, not only keeping it cool and blocking out light (which would turn it rancid) but imbuing the fat with its own minerals so that it takes on a subtle flavour unique to that place.

You can't, of course, recreate that special product, but you can make something similar, and very delicious. Lardo should be sliced gossamer-thin and can be eaten raw with a small amount of olive oil or, as I particularly recommend, wrapped around freshly steamed asparagus so that it becomes translucent and melting.

Makes about 500g

A slab of thick pork back fat, skin on, about 1kg

For the cure
250g coarse sea salt
15g black peppercorns, freshly cracked
20g juniper berries, bruised

10 garlic cloves, peeled and very finely chopped, almost to a paste
3–4 sprigs of rosemary or thyme
5g bay leaves, finely shredded

Equipment
Ziplock food bag

For the cure, put the salt, cracked pepper, juniper berries, garlic and herbs in a bowl and mix well. Put the pork fat in a ziplock food bag (in which it will fit snugly coated in the cure) and pour in the cure. Seal the bag.

Gently massage the cure around all the sides of the pork fat (the cure mix must be in constant contact with the surface of the fat). Put the ziplock bag into a black plastic bag to stop light getting to it and refrigerate for 3–6 months. Although not typical, I place a weight on top as it gives the lardo a pleasing density.

When the lardo is ready, remove the outer rind of skin in a single sheet (use this to add body to a soup or stew, placing it on top). Slice the lardo extremely thinly and serve. Lardo will keep, wrapped in black plastic, in the fridge indefinitely.

Coppa

TECHNIQUE	Dry-curing
CURING TIME	Minimum 8 weeks, plus 2 days

Coppa is a classic Italian cured meat made from the 'eye' of muscle that extends from the shoulder of a pig into the neck. The piece of meat itself is also called the coppa, which roughly translates as nape (as in neck). At River Cottage we usually remove it from a spare rib joint before we mince the rest of the meat for sausages or salami. The coppa is pretty easy to remove – it's simply a case of seaming out (i.e. dividing) a set of muscles. Once located, it will practically show you where to make the cuts (see pp.64 and 67). Alternatively a good butcher will do this for you.

The curing method requires salt at 3% of the weight of the meat and 1 day's curing per kg of meat, or you could apply the salt-box method (see p.98). The following recipe is based on an average uncured coppa weight of about 2kg.

Makes 1 coppa (about 1.4kg)

1 free-range pork coppa (see above),
   about 2kg
An ox bung casing (lower intestine)

For the cure
60g PDV salt
10g white peppercorns, freshly ground
20g black peppercorns, freshly cracked
1 tsp ground cinnamon
2–3 cloves, crushed
20 juniper berries, bruised
2–3 bay leaves, shredded
A glass of white wine

Equipment
Ziplock food bag
Food-standard tray
Butcher's string
Meat slicer (optional)

Put all the ingredients for the cure in a bowl and mix thoroughly. Put the pork coppa into a ziplock food bag, pour in the cure and seal the bag. Massage the cure into the meat so that it gets a liberal covering.

Put the bag on a tray and place in the fridge. Leave the coppa to cure in the fridge for the allotted time (1 day per kg), giving it a gentle massage every other day. On the penultimate day, put the ox bung casing to soak in cold water.

Take the meat out of the bag and wash off the cure under a cold running tap. Wipe it dry. I like to wipe a clean cloth soaked in wine over the meat at this point because it gives a nice acidic, clean surface to the coppa, which will protect it.

Place the meat in the ox bung casing (just like putting on a sock). Secure both ends with string, then tie along the length of the coppa using the butcher's knot (see pp.148–9). Prick with a sterilised pin so that any air bubbles will be released; this will allow the skin to shrink back with the meat during the drying-out process.

Put the coppa back in the fridge and leave to cure for 8–10 weeks or until it has lost 30% of its original weight. Try and maintain an average temperature of around 10°C or so (which should be possible in a domestic fridge).

When it is ready, the coppa will be firm to the touch with a little bit of give. Slice it thinly and remove the casing before eating. It is excellent served with thinly sliced beetroot.

Variations

There are several ways to customise your coppa using different ingredients. You can replace the cinnamon, cloves, juniper and bay with spices such as cayenne and paprika, or try a mellow fennel seed version.

Gravadlax with beetroot

TECHNIQUE	Dry-curing/brine hybrid
CURING TIME	Minimum 3 days

This is a classic, adapted from *The River Cottage Fish Book*. The beetroot in the cure is my addition. The vegetable has no real curing properties but it has plenty of flavour, of course, and immense visual impact. Coloured with the beetroot, the salmon is reminiscent of a sunset watched from a tropical island.

Serves 10–15

2 sides (large fillets) of wild salmon,
    about 1kg in total

For the cure
100g caster sugar
75g PDV salt
15g black or white peppercorns,
    or a mixture, coarsely ground
A large bunch of dill, coarse stalks
    removed, finely chopped
2–3 cooked beetroot, peeled and grated

Equipment
Food-standard tray
Kitchen tweezers

Remove the pin bones that run down the centre of salmon fillets with tweezers.

Mix all the ingredients for the cure together in a bowl. Place a good handful of the cure on the bottom of a food-standard tray. Lay the first salmon fillet on top, skin side down, then cover with more cure. Top with the second fillet, skin side down, and cover again with cure. Put a board on top, weigh down and place in the fridge.

Leave the fish to cure for at least 3 days (for smaller fillets) and up to 7 days (for really big fillets from a 5kg or larger salmon). Every day, turn the 'fillet sandwich' over and baste the fish in its accumulated juices, then replace the weight.

When the fish is cured, rinse the fillets and pat them dry. The outside of the fillets will be stained purple and will have a wonderful gradient of purple and orange along the thin slices. Serve with lightly buttered rye bread.

Note: Unsliced gravadlax can be wrapped and kept in the fridge for up to 10 days.

Prosciutto

TECHNIQUES	Total immersion method, air-drying
CURING TIME	Minimum 12 months

This is the start of a wonderful journey, one that will take you all the way back to the beginning of curing culture, and involve over a year of your life. Of all the recipes I teach at River Cottage, this is the one which really convinces people that they can produce an authentic, traditional cured product, no matter where they live or how inexperienced they may be.

Dry-curing and air-drying a leg of pork will test your nerve because it is such a long time before you get to the pay-off. It will be a roller coaster of emotions, triggering the worries you'd expect when meat is unrefrigerated, covered in mould and, from the outside, not appetising in appearance. Let those doubts come and go. Follow these simple instructions, be vigilant, confident and patient, and – in time – you will create one of the finest examples of cured meat there is.

Although this follows an authentic method, you shouldn't expect to produce something that tastes just like genuine Parma ham, or Ibérico pata negra jamón. The breeds of pig used to make those hams – as well as their diet, terrain and climate – are unique. However, if you use good British pork, from a traditional breed such as Berkshire, Saddleback or Gloucester Old Spot, you will produce a fantastic ham with a quality and flavour that reflects your particular environment.

I always dry-cure prosciutto on the bone and slice it in the traditional way. However, I understand that you might want to slice large rounds unobstructed, so I've given instructions on how to remove the bone after curing on pp.160–3.

Makes 1 prosciutto (about 7kg)

A leg of free-range pork, bone in and trotter attached
2 x 25kg bags PDV salt (one for submerging the ham in and the other to act as a weight placed on top of the ham)
About 100ml malt vinegar

Equipment
Heavy-duty scales (up to 10kg)
Large plastic (or wooden) food-standard box and wooden board
Butcher's hook
Jambon sac (optional)
Meat slicer (optional)

Weigh the leg of pork before you begin, as this determines the length of time it needs to be immersed in the salt. The meat requires 3 days' salting per kg. So, for example, a leg weighing 5kg will need to be in salt for 15 days.

Before you place the leg of pork in the salt, remove any flaps of skin or oxidised parts of meat where blood has coagulated. Try to make the surface of the meat as clean and even as possible. It also pays to massage the leg from the trotter end to the thicker end, as this will release any residual blood that may be left in the femoral artery. Blood has a negative effect in curing meats. Rub the pork with a clean cloth doused in malt vinegar. The main advantage of keeping the trotter on is that you can then hang the leg for air-drying by the Achilles tendon on a butcher's hook. In addition, you won't be exposing an extra bit of flesh, which reduces the risk of spoilage, or attracting flies.

Have your chosen container ready (see p.100). It is better to have the box in situ now, because, once it contains the ham and salt, it will be a real hernia job trying to move it. The best site for the salting to take place is off the floor in an outhouse or in a cool, dry larder or pantry.

Pour a layer of salt about 4cm deep over the base of the container and place the pork leg on top. Add the rest of the salt, making sure every bit of the leg is covered and it is completely submerged beneath at least 4cm of salt. If the leg is particularly large, it may be the case that more salt is required to complete the job. This will look and feel like an excessive amount of salt but it is a guaranteed ratio that will work. If you use a plastic box you have the advantage of being able to see if the ham is touching the side of the box, without being surrounded by salt. Lift the leg slightly at that point and allow the salt to encase it by giving it a gentle prod. If you use a wooden box, just make sure there is enough clearance around the leg when you put it in for it to be completely enveloped in the salt.

Find a wooden chopping board that fits neatly inside the box and place it on top of the salt-covered pork. Put a large weight on top. It has to be a significant weight. I use a spare 25kg bag of salt (still contained in the bag) or an old potato weight (56lb) for this purpose. The weight helps to drive the cure in as well as give the ham that classic Parma/prosciutto shape. Make a note of the date your ham is due to come out of the salt. A day either side of this date may not be too critical to the overall final taste but try and stick to it.

When you have salted the ham for the allotted time, remove it from the box and wash it thoroughly with fresh cold water to remove the salt. Rub the whole joint with malt vinegar then hang it in your air-drying spot for up to 12 months. In warm weather, wrap it loosely in a muslin 'jambon sac' (see p.52) so that flies won't be able to get to it but the air will be able to move over it and you will still be able to see the ham through the thin muslin. If you wrap it too tight it will still allow flies to lay eggs through it. If there is a cold snap, you don't really want the ham to freeze – it halts the curing process, although that will continue once it warms up again. Freezing is actually unlikely, due to the amount of salt present in the ham, but if temperatures get very low, you might want to move it to a slightly warmer place, or even the fridge.

It is important that the ham doesn't dry too fast or it will be 'sealed' on the outside, and moisture won't be able to escape, but you do want a crust to gradually form on the outside that will protect it. To keep the drying slow, the ham must not be allowed to get too warm (i.e. go above 26°C). Air circulation is really the most crucial thing – it is no use trying to do this in a stagnant environment as this will attract the wrong moulds.

The first time you do this, let the ham hang for the full 12 months (by which time it should have lost 30% of its original weight). Any less than this and you will just be cheating yourself on overall taste.

When it comes to the time to sample your ham, remove it from the muslin, if used. It should be firm and have a covering of mould over it. There may be a slight smell of unpasteurised cheese about it, or something a bit musty. Don't worry about this; it is perfectly normal. I take a nailbrush and dip it in malt vinegar at this point to remove the mould from the area where I want to try the ham – usually from the exposed area of meat near the aitchbone but it doesn't really matter. The mould won't harm you but it's not necessarily the best part.

Using a sharp knife, carefully remove the hard, crusty exterior to expose the wonderful meat just underneath. Slice the ham as finely as you can and enjoy its deliciousness as you reflect on the passing year.

Note: Don't add any herbs or spices to the ham before it goes into the salt. It is better to add flavour much later on, after eating some of the cured ham for the first time. After the first slices have been taken off, exposing some of the cured leg, you can create a covering paste consisting of pork lard and flour. The Italians call this a *strutto* and it acts as a protective barrier, allowing the ham to continue to mature. You can add flavourings such as coriander, chilli and black pepper to this paste – they won't affect the cure but will inform the first few layers of meat underneath the *strutto*.

Variation

If you want to practise all the elements of curing a piece of pork in this way but don't want to go straight to the expense of a whole leg, then you can apply the same technique to a chump joint. Follow the same method, and weight/curing time ratio, but expect it to be ready to eat in around 4 months.

Boning an air-dried ham

Traditionally, Parma and prosciutto hams are cured with the aitchbone removed but with the femur still in. The aitchbone is part of the pelvis that sits on top of the femur bone at the thick end of the leg and creates a classic 'ball and socket joint'. It takes a certain amount of skill to remove it but can be done with a bit of patience – or you could ask your butcher to do it for you.

The first time you cure a leg, I would suggest you leave the aitchbone in, because it offers that extra bit of protection and leaves less flesh exposed. However, leaving it in does cause some difficulties later on when it comes to slicing the leg – it will act as an obstruction. You certainly won't be able to use a meat slicer with the aitchbone still in – nor, for that matter, will you be able to slice lovely large rounds of ham with the femur still running through it. You will just need to get proficient at shaving off shards with a sharp knife – just as they do in Italy and Spain.

To remove the aitchbone before curing, you will need a flexible boning knife to work your way underneath the bone. The technique is illustrated on p.74. Once you've traced the outline of the aitchbone it is a matter of prising it away from the femur and connective tissue. To the first timer this will be fiddly and the addition of working with a sharp knife adds to the jeopardy. Take your time and always make sure the ham is resting steadily against the board. Rather like shucking an oyster shell, this technique will become second nature with practice.

If you want to create a boneless air-dried ham, perfect for slicing on a meat slicer, you can remove the femur during the drying process at around 6 months. If you attempt to remove the bone too early in the drying process, the ham will never regain its shape and the space created by removing the bone won't close. If you leave it too late then the ham will be so hard that it will be impossible to get the gouge in. Generally the hams that I bone out are 6–8 months along their curing journey. This is quite a large window, I know: the best way to judge it is by pressing hard on the outside of your ham and feeling if there is some 'give', which slowly comes back to shape after a while. This is the time to bone it.

You will need a butcher's saw and a hand bone gouge, which looks like a large metal shoehorn and has a bevelled end and a rounded shaft (pic 1). It is the same bit of kit that they use in hip operations.

With the aitchbone removed before you place the leg in salt, you already have one point of entry for the hand bone gouge. However, you still need to expose and release the other end which is just above the knee. There is a recognisable point on the cut surface of the leg which indicates where to make the incision. It looks like

Boning an air-dried ham at around 6 months

(continued overleaf)

Boning an air-dried ham (continued)

two small peaks either side of a dip (pic 2). If it isn't apparent to the naked eye then you should be able to feel for it. You should be able to make a cut here all the way through the leg so that the knuckle below the knee is removed. Don't worry if this sounds too complicated – you could always choose a point near to where you think the knee is and use the saw to cut through the bone. It's just a bit crude and passes some bone dust around the meat.

Take the tip of a knife and start to prise away the flesh at the top end of the femur (pic 3) and at the other end so that you can insert the tip of the gouge. Don't go in too deep with the knife as this will cause criss-cross marks to run visibly through the meat which will ruin the look of any rounds sliced off.

Now, with some effort, you should be able to force the end of the gouge along the length of the bone (pic 4) in order to separate it from the muscles and pull it free; the shape of the gouge means you won't leave too much meat on the bone. Eventually you should be able to work all around the bone (pic 5) so that it can be removed completely with a bit of a twist and a pull (pic 6). Often the knee cap is still in place, and this should be located and removed. It looks and feels like a hard circular dome just under the skin close to where you made your cut.

Now you have a tunnel where the bone used to be, which needs to be sealed up (pic 7). Don't be tempted to pack this space with salt – it will make your ham far too salty. Instead, devise a way to press the ham so that the gap becomes sealed. At River Cottage we have specially rigged-up boxes which we use to press hams. They are made from pine and consist of a frame deep enough to hold a big ham with slats top and bottom, which encase the ham. The slats are tightened on to the ham with pieces of wood running across the top and bottom, using two threaded bolts and a couple of wing nuts. This get-up is typically River Cottage in the sense it is ever so slightly 'rustic', but it absolutely works. In much the same manner, here I've used an apple press (pic 8); two pieces of wood held tightly with clamps would function in the same way. The ham should be ready after 24 hours in the press. You can then carry on air-drying it for the rest of the year as it was.

Goat violin

TECHNIQUES	Dry-curing, air-drying
CURING TIME	Minimum 2 months

Goat is such an underestimated meat, with many uses beyond the wonderful curried goat. It can also be a very sustainable and ethical choice. At River Cottage we are lucky enough to work with James Whetlor of Cabrito who supplies us with meat from young male goats, by-products of the goat dairy industry. Goats like these would normally be killed at birth, but when fed up and well looked after, billy goat meat can be a delicacy on a par with rose veal (the corresponding by-product of the bovine dairy industry). Young goat meat is extremely lean with a milky pinkness and a musky, gamey smell. These notes carry through to the cured meat, although the colour becomes darker.

This recipe owes much to a northern Italian prosciutto-style, dry-cured recipe, *violino di capra*. Traditionally the cured goat leg is passed around a table of diners who hold it like a violin and slice off the meat using a long knife as if it were a bow.

As goat leg is very lean, it takes a shorter time to cure and dry than a pork leg and it needs less salt – just 3% of the weight of the leg. This cure method is less aggressive than the salt-box method used for a prosciutto ham.

Makes about 1kg
1 goat leg, about 2–3kg

For the cure
About 60g PDV salt (i.e. 3% of the
    weight of the goat leg)
100g demerara sugar
4 garlic cloves, peeled and crushed
10g juniper berries, bruised
12g black peppercorns, freshly cracked
3 sprigs of thyme
3 sprigs of rosemary
5 bay leaves

Equipment
Ziplock food bag
Food-standard tray
Butcher's hook and string
Meat slicer (optional)

For the cure, mix all the ingredients together in a bowl. Put the goat leg into a ziplock food bag and pour the cure over it. Seal the bag. Make sure the leg is covered on all sides with the cure and, if the femur bone is exposed at the top end, pay particular attention to getting some cure in and around the ball of the bone. Massage the cure into the meat, making sure it is evenly distributed.

Place the ziplock bag in a tray or suitable container and leave to cure in the fridge, allowing 1 day for every kg. The leg should be massaged or at least turned once or twice in order to redistribute the cure.

After the allotted curing time, remove the goat leg from the bag and rinse off the cure under a cold running tap. Pat it dry with a clean tea towel. Discard the liquid that has collected in the ziplock bag. Once cured, the leg should feel firmer and have a darker hue to it.

Now hang the goat leg in suitable air-drying conditions (see p.103), with a good flow of air, 60–80% humidity and a temperature that is somewhere between 10 and 18°C, for 2–5 months.

Serve the cured goat finely sliced, like a prosciutto, with figs.

Variation

Lamb violin A fairly small leg of lamb, weighing 2–3kg, can be used instead of the goat leg for this recipe.

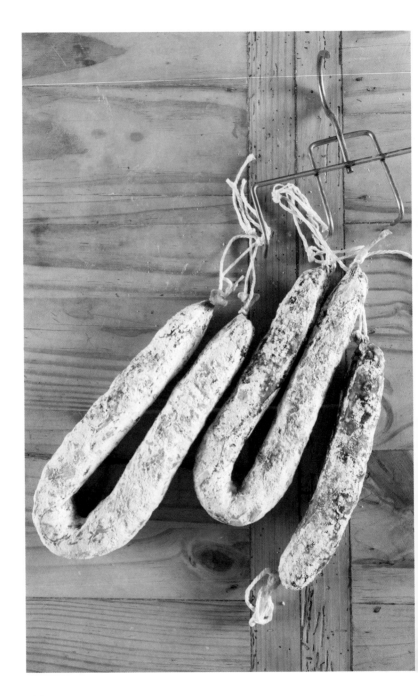

Salami

TECHNIQUES	Fermentation, air-drying
CURING TIME	Minimum 6 weeks

This method of curing meat is perhaps the oldest. The meat is allowed to ferment and dry out over a period of time, resulting in a form of sausage that doesn't need to be cooked. The cure is integrated fully with the meat, rather than being applied to the surface, so the meat needs to be minced or finely chopped to allow the cure to work effectively. The ratio of salt to the overall weight of the other ingredients must be a minimum of 2% in order to cure the meat effectively but not much more than this to avoid over-salting.

The full technique for filling and tying salami is described and illustrated on pp.88–92. It is simple enough, but easier if you get someone to help you.

Makes about 10 salami

Several lengths of beef runners or
  beef middle casings
2.6kg boneless shoulder or hand
  of free-range pork
400g back fat (see p.81)
1–2 garlic cloves, peeled and very
  finely chopped
40g black peppercorns, freshly cracked
1–2 glasses of red wine
60g PDV salt

Equipment
Meat mincer
Sausage filler
Butcher's hooks and string
Meat slicer (optional)

Soak the casings for at least 2 hours in cold water.

Mince the pork shoulder or hand using the coarse (8–10mm) plate of your mincer and place in a bowl. Cut the back fat into 2mm dice and add to the meat. Now add the garlic, cracked pepper, wine and salt. Mix the ingredients together thoroughly by hand.

Pack the mixture into the barrel of your sausage stuffer and fit a medium nozzle on the end. Load the casing on to the sausage stuffer, tie the end with string and fill the casing as described and shown on pp.88–92, to form sausages about 30cm long, packing tightly and ensuring there are no air pockets. Secure the other end of the casing with a second piece of string.

The natural casings are inclined to bow into a horseshoe shape. I tie the string at the ends of the salami into loops, then slip both loops on to one hook and hang them like this. However, if you prefer straight salami, suspend them from one end only and they will straighten up. To begin with, you will need to hang the salami in a warm place, ideally 25–27°C, to enable incubation of the bacteria and facilitate fermentation.

After 12 hours in this environment, move the salami to your dry-curing spot, which should be between 12 and 18°C with a humidity level of approximately 70% and a constant circulation of air (see p.103). Make sure the salami are not touching a wall, or each other, and they are not in direct sunlight. Over the coming weeks, test the pH to ensure it is below 4.5. A white mould should form on the casings, indicating that this level has been reached.

The salami may take anything from 6–10 weeks to mature, depending on the conditions and, indeed, on how you like them. They can be sampled as soon as they are fairly firm to the touch and dry-looking, but they will continue to dry out and harden until they are practically rock hard.

When the salami reach the stage you like, wipe off any mould from the outside with a cloth soaked in vinegar, then rub the surface with a little olive oil. Transfer the salami to the fridge.

Serve your salami in slices 2–3mm thick. If you prefer, peel off the ring of casing from each slice before eating, although it is perfectly safe to eat.

Variations

Fennel seeds and grated orange zest make a wonderful addition to this mix and go really well with the pork. Alternatively, try them in a venison salami: in this case you still have to include some pork fat in the mix as venison is a very lean meat. A ratio of 3 parts venison to 1 part pork fat works well.

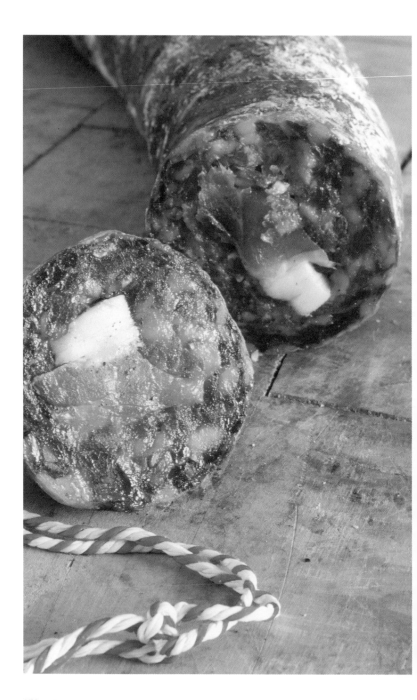

Chorizo

TECHNIQUES	Fermentation, air-drying
CURING TIME	Minimum 6 weeks

There are probably hundreds of recipes for chorizo. Throughout Spain, and indeed Mexico, families have been handing down their own recipes for generations. The meat is flavoured with a spice mix, usually largely informed by paprika, but which can also include fiery cayenne or naga chilli, which will send it off the Scoville scale (the scale that chilli heat is measured in).

This recipe is for a salami-style chorizo, made with a fairly eclectic blend of spices that can be altered to suit your own heat threshold. It also includes pieces of cured loin of pork, which provide a nice contrast, both texturally and visually. I've added smoked paprika to the mix, to give it a more subtle smokiness. Alternatively, you could use ordinary paprika and cold-smoke the salami yourself (see p.114), after it has had 2 weeks or so of normal air-drying.

Makes about 20 medium chorizo

3–4 lengths of beef runner casings
5kg boneless shoulder or hand of
   free-range pork, with about
   20% fat (measured roughly by eye)
1kg cured pork loin (see back bacon
   variation, p.142)
100g PDV salt (i.e. 2% of the weight
   of the pork shoulder or hand)
125g smoked hot paprika
70g sweet paprika (unsmoked)
15g cayenne pepper
50g fennel seeds, lightly toasted
10 garlic cloves, peeled and
   finely chopped
1–2 glasses red wine

Equipment
Meat mincer
Sausage stuffer
Butcher's hooks and string
Meat slicer (optional)

Soak the casings for at least 2 hours in cold water.

Mince the pork shoulder or hand using the coarse (8–10mm) plate of your mincer and place in a bowl. Cut the pork loin into small cubes and add to the minced meat

with all the other ingredients except the wine. Mix thoroughly, using your hands, so that the flavourings are well distributed throughout the mixture. Now add enough wine to bind the mixture (but not too much or it will leach out of the skins later, carrying flavour with it, and also some of the crucial salt).

Pack the mixture into the sausage stuffer and fit a medium nozzle on the end. Load the casing on to the sausage stuffer, tie the end with string and fill the casing as described and shown on pp.88–92, to form sausages about 30cm long, packing tightly and ensuring there are no air pockets. Secure the other end of the casing with string.

To begin with, you will need to hang the chorizo in a warm place, ideally 25–27°C, to enable incubation of the bacteria and facilitate fermentation.

After 12 hours in this environment, move the chorizo to your dry-curing spot, which should be between 12 and 18°C with a humidity level of approximately 70% and a constant circulation of air (see p.103). Make sure the chorizo are not touching a wall, or each other, and they are not in direct sunlight. Over the coming weeks, test the pH to ensure it is below 4.5. Allow 6–10 weeks for the chorizo to cure if you want to eat it raw. Serve cut into thin slices.

Note: Should you want to, you can cook with the chorizo soon after mixing rather than leave it to cure. Try crumbling it over fish before baking or putting it into casings and cooking like a sausage to serve with scrambled eggs. There will be an extra saltiness to it, but not to its detriment. Just hold back on additional seasonings in the dish you are preparing.

Chorizo Scotch egg

This is a brilliant way to use up any leftover chorizo mix. Boil a medium egg for 6 minutes and allow it to cool. Shell the egg, wrap it in a portion of chorizo mix and roll it in flour, beaten egg and breadcrumbs respectively. Deep-fry in hot oil for 5 minutes or until golden brown. On slicing it open, the pork should be cooked through and the egg yolk still runny.

Cotechino

TECHNIQUES	Fermentation, air-drying
CURING TIME	Minimum 5 days

Making this Italian cured sausage is a labour of love because it involves dicing a considerable amount of back fat and pork rind into small pieces, which is a fairly tricky operation. The fat slips in your fingers and the rind is tough and difficult to cut, but it is definitely worth the effort. The meat should carry a good amount of fat, with additional finely chopped pork rind mixed in. I like to use the flavourful rind from a piece of streaky bacon, or the skin removed from an aged piece of lardo (see p.151); the mix of fatty flavours gives a wonderful salty-sticky quality to the cured sausage. This classic recipe is adapted from *The River Cottage Meat Book*.

Makes 3–4 cotechino

Natural sausage casings: for a salami-
 style cotechino use ox middles
 (5–10cm wide); or for a larger
 haggis-style cotechino use
 ox bung (about 15cm wide)
1kg boneless shoulder or hand of
 free-range pork
400g pork back fat
600g pork rind

For the cure

50g fine salt
A glass of red wine
2 garlic cloves, peeled and finely
 chopped
1 tsp black or mixed peppercorns,
 freshly ground
A few gratings of fresh nutmeg
1 tsp ground cinnamon
3–4 cloves, ground
1 tsp ground mace
A good pinch of dried thyme
4 dried bay leaves

Equipment

Meat mincer
Sausage stuffer
Butcher's hooks and string

Soak the sausage casings overnight in cold water.

Mince the meat using the coarse (8–10mm) plate of your mincer and place in a bowl. Dice the pork fat and rind into small pieces, add to the meat and mix well.

Mix the cure ingredients together in a bowl. Add the combined meat, fat and rind and mix thoroughly by hand.

Pack the mixture into the sausage stuffer and fit a medium nozzle on the end. Load the casing on to the sausage stuffer, tie the end with string and fill the casing as shown and described on pp.88–92, to form sausages about 10cm long, packing the mixture tightly and ensuring there are no air pockets. Secure the other end of the casing with string.

Hang the cotechino in a dry, airy place, such as a draughty outbuilding or covered porch, making sure they do not touch a wall, or each other (see p.103). They will be ready to cook and eat after about 5 days but are perhaps at their best at around 15–20 days. By about 40 days they will be pretty dry and hard.

If you wish to keep the cotechino any longer, vac-pack or wrap in cling film and refrigerate, and they will keep for another month or so. Alternatively, freeze them for up to a year.

To cook a cotechino, immerse it fully in a pan of cold water and slowly bring to a simmer. Cook gently for about 1½ hours for thin sausages (i.e. stuffed middles) or 2½ hours for fat ones (i.e. stuffed bung).

Drain the cotechino and cut into thick slices. It is delicious served hot on a bed of warm Puy lentils dressed with olive oil, salt and pepper.

Szechuan-cured pork loin

TECHNIQUES	Dry-curing, air-drying
CURING TIME	Minimum 4 days

This uses a boneless loin of pork with a layer of back fat still attached – essentially a rack of invertebrate pork chops. The loin can be cured as a whole or in shorter sections. The curing time will be the same whatever the length, as it is the thickness not length that determines how long it needs in the cure. This cure with its oriental twist is inspired by my friend Mark Diacono, who grows his own Szechuan pepper and is constantly inviting me to wonder at its unique, tongue-tingling flavour.

Makes about 50 rashers

1kg piece of boneless free-range pork
    loin, with a layer of back fat

For the cure
30g coarse sea salt
50g Szechuan pepper, roughly ground
30g black peppercorns, toasted
    and cracked

Equipment
Ziplock food bag
Food-standard tray
Butcher's hooks and string

Mix all the ingredients for the cure together in a bowl. Put the pork loin into a ziplock bag and add the cure, massaging it all over the meat. Seal the bag, excluding as much air as possible. Place the bag on a tray or in the salad drawer of your fridge.

Leave the pork to cure in the fridge for 3 days per kg, giving it a gentle massage to redistribute the cure evenly every day. After the allotted time, remove the pork from the bag and wash off the cure under cold running water. Pat the meat dry and allow it to dry completely – placing it, uncovered, back in the fridge overnight is a good way to do this. The cured pork is now ready to slice and fry (like back bacon).

For a more pronounced peppery flavour, you can dust the surface of the cured loin with extra Szechuan and black pepper. Tie along the joint using the butcher's knot (see pp.148–9) and hang it in your air-drying spot (see p.103) for 3–4 weeks or until it has lost 30% of the original weight. It can then be served raw, in thin slices.

Variation

Filletto For a quicker version, use pork tenderloin (a mini loin without fat).

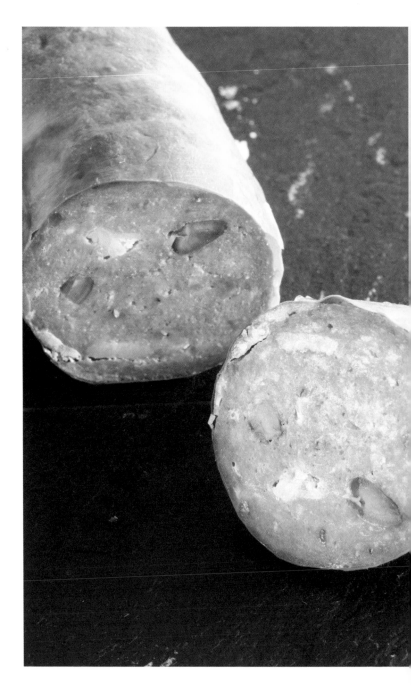

Mortadella

TECHNIQUE	Poaching (no curing)
COOKING TIME	Minimum 50 minutes

Comprising a mix of meat and fat, which is processed to a smooth paste, this is an emulsified sausage rather than a salami. Instead of being air-dried, it is poached and cooled before slicing. This recipe is from my friend Robin Rea of Rusty Pig.

Makes 1 mortadella

1 beef middle casing
500g boneless free-range pork belly
500g pork back fat
2 garlic cloves, peeled and minced
15g coarse sea salt
1 tsp black peppercorns, freshly ground
1 tsp ground mace
½ tsp freshly grated nutmeg

½ tsp ground coriander
25g shelled pistachio nuts

Equipment
Meat mincer
Sausage stuffer
Butcher's string
Meat temperature probe

Soak the beef casing overnight in cold water.

Mince the belly and back fat separately, through the fine (3mm) plate of the mincer.

Put the belly in a bowl and add the garlic, salt, pepper, mace, nutmeg and coriander. Mix thoroughly, then pass again through the fine plate on the mincer. Place the seasoned meat and the fat in a bowl and refrigerate for at least 30 minutes.

Put the chilled meat and fat into a food processor and process until smooth, then transfer the mixture to a chilled bowl and mix in the pistachios.

Pack the mix into the sausage stuffer and fit the widest nozzle on the end. Load the beef casing on to the sausage stuffer, tie off with a double knot and fill the casing so it has no air gaps, then secure the other end as shown and described on pp.88–92.

Lower the sausage into a pot of water and heat slowly. Cook below simmering (at about 75°C) for 45 minutes to 1 hour. The internal temperature of the mortadella should reach 65°C, which you can measure with a meat temperature probe.

Meanwhile, fill a large bowl with cold water and ice cubes. Remove the cooked mortadella from the pan and immerse in the ice bath to cool quickly, then drain. Serve the mortadella cut into thin slices. It will keep in the fridge for a week.

Guanciale

TECHNIQUES	Dry-curing, air-drying
CURING TIME	Minimum 4 weeks

The first time I tried this dry-cured air-dried pig's cheek it was simply fried in its own juices with a splash of balsamic vinegar. It has made a lasting impression on me and whenever I think about curing meat, memories of that first tasting always come to mind, like a marked page in a well-thumbed book.

The jowl of a pig is a wonderful cut. Combining fat and lean meat, it is soft and yielding before curing (guanciale translates as 'pillow') but, once cured, it takes on firmness and incredible character. It can be used to flavour soups, stews and pasta sauces, like bacon, or sliced thinly and eaten raw like pancetta.

Sadly, because there appears to be a real stumbling block when it comes to 'face meat', the majority of meat from a pig's head is used to make pet food. Perhaps it makes the link between living animal and food on the plate all too clear for some. I prefer to make the best use of those cuts and to be upfront about what they are. At River Cottage, we've taken to referring to this particular product as 'face bacon', to really hammer it home.

Makes about 60 rashers
2 pig's cheeks, about 1kg in total

For the cure
About 300g PDV salt (i.e. 3% of the weight of the pig's cheeks), or, if using the salt-box method, see p.98
60g black peppercorns, freshly cracked

Equipment
Kitchen blowtorch (optional)
Ziplock food bag
Butcher's hooks

First you need to burn away any residual hair on the pig cheeks. Singe the cheeks with a kitchen blowtorch or over a gas ring, then scrape away the burnt hair with a knife.

Now remove any glands from around the back of the cheeks. They are part of the lymphatic system (which cleans the blood) and won't do you any harm if eaten but they are greyish, pappy and unappealing.

Mix the ingredients for the cure together in a bowl, then transfer to a ziplock bag.

Put the cheeks into the bag and distribute the cure evenly, so that it covers them. Squeeze out as much air as possible, seal the bag and place on a plastic tray.

Place the tray in the fridge. Let the cheeks cure, allowing 3 days per 500g (in this case, 6 days), redistributing the cure once or twice as it becomes more liquid.

Remove the cheeks and wash off the cure under cold running water, then pat them dry with a clean tea towel. I like to then dust the dry-cured cheeks with more cracked black pepper.

Hang the cured pig's cheeks on butcher's hooks to air-dry in appropriate conditions (see p.103) for 3–5 weeks.

When ready, remove the rind and slice the guanciale thinly to eat raw, or cut into pieces to add to soups, stews and pasta sauces, or fry slices like bacon rashers.

Variations

For a sweeter flavour, use the basic River Cottage dry cure (see p.96). This recipe also works exceptionally well with duck breasts, using the same ratios and timings to create a wonderful duck prosciutto.

Spalla and speck

TECHNIQUES	Dry-curing, cold-smoking (optional), air-drying
CURING TIME	Minimum 6 months

This might sound like a sequel TV series starring the offspring of Mork and Mindy but it is in fact is a wonderful duo of cured meats produced from the same cut of pork, the difference being that speck is cold-smoked and spalla is not. Their flavours are quite distinct – the smokiness of speck originating from the traditional storage of cured meat in chimneys during the warmer months.

Spalla is traditionally made by keeping the cut on the bone, but I like to remove the bone first so it can easily be sliced. It is very much like dry-cured, air-dried ham (see p.156) but with the bonus of being ready to eat sooner. It will have the look and texture of a prosciutto but, because of its accelerated ascent to curedom, it won't carry the same complex flavours. However, it will still taste wonderful.

Speck shares the same start in life as spalla but after boning and curing it is cold-smoked before air-drying. It is considered to be less refined than a dry-cured ham because it comes from the forequarter of the pig, not the leg, but I love it – especially its complex spice and herb flavours applied through the cure.

Makes 1 spalla or speck (about 2.8kg)

A boneless shoulder of free-range
   pork, about 4kg

For the cure

About 120g fine sea salt (i.e. 3% of
   the weight of the pork shoulder)
½ tsp English mustard
½ tsp freshly grated nutmeg
50g dried juniper berries, finely ground
50g allspice, freshly ground
50g black peppercorns, freshly ground
85g dark brown sugar
10 bay leaves, shredded

Equipment
Ziplock food bag
Butcher's hooks and string
Cold smoker for speck

Place the meat, skin side down, on a board and remove any flaps of loose skin or meat. You are looking to get the surface of the meat as even as possible so it will cure at a uniform rate.

Mix all the cure ingredients together in a bowl. Grab half of the cure and scatter it in the bottom of a ziplock bag. Place the pork on top, skin side down, then apply the rest of the cure, massaging it gently into the meat and making sure that the sides are also covered. Seal the ziplock bag.

Leave the meat to cure in a cool place for the equivalent of 3 days per kg weight. If you can find room in your fridge, all the better. Redistribute the cure in the bag every other day so that it is kept in close proximity to the meat.

After the allotted time (12 days for a 4kg shoulder), wash the cure off the meat under cold running water and pat it dry with a clean tea towel. Allow the meat to sit in the fridge for a day or so.

Roll and tie along the joint using the butcher's knot (see pp.148–9).

If you want to make speck, at this stage fire up your cold smoker and cold-smoke the meat gently for 4–8 hours.

Either way – smoked or not – air-dry the meat as you would an air-dried ham (see pp.158–9), until it has lost 30% of its original weight, which can take anywhere from 6–12 months. Serve spalla or speck cut into thin slices.

Venison biltong

TECHNIQUES	Dry-curing, wet-curing, air-drying
CURING TIME	Minimum 10 days

This flavour-packed cured snack from South Africa is pretty close to jerky in its method. It is quite brittle and hard to begin with but, after a few challenging chews, it starts to soften and relent, allowing all those fantastic flavours to fill your mouth. On the odd occasion when the River Cottage team is allowed out of the county, we can often be seen munching on sticks of home-cured biltong on the train to London.

Each 500g makes 4–6 strips

A whole small or ½ large haunch
   of venison

For the cure

2 tbsp PDV salt
2 tbsp soft dark brown sugar
1 tbsp coriander seeds, roasted
   and ground
1 tbsp black peppercorns, freshly
   cracked
3 tbsp malt vinegar

Equipment
Food-standard tray
Butcher's hooks and string

Prepare the meat by seaming out (i.e. dividing) the leg into individual muscles. Only use the meat which you can clearly define as being long-grained (the rest is ideal for salami).

Using a sharp knife, slice the meat along the grain into long steaks, about 2–3cm thick, removing any sinew and fat as you go. You need 500g meat. A leg will give you more than you require, so divide the rest into batches and freeze it for future biltong-making or for venison salami.

For the cure, mix the salt, sugar, coriander and cracked pepper together thoroughly in a bowl. Scatter a layer of this cure mixture evenly in a large food-standard tray, then add the venison steaks. Cover the meat evenly with the remaining cure, rubbing it in well. Now add the malt vinegar, sprinkling it evenly over both sides of the venison steaks.

Cover the tray and place in the fridge. Allow to cure for 6 hours, turning the meat and rubbing in the mixture again after 2 hours.

Remove the meat from the tray. Shake off any loose seasoning and carefully pat the meat dry with a tea towel. Hang each strip of biltong individually from a hook, using a piece of string. Leave it to dry in a cool, dry, dark and airy place (at 10°C) until semi-dried – about 10 days.

You can then finish your biltong off in a very low oven. I am fortunate to have a wonderful Esse stove at home, which has two oven compartments and I hang the biltong strips in the bottom warming oven, using butcher's hooks. If your cooker doesn't have a warming oven, hang the meat from the top shelf of your oven on its lowest setting. If you think that may still be too hot, leave the oven door slightly open. It will take about 4–6 hours to dry. When finished, the biltong should be so dry that it will splinter when bent in two.

Alternatively, if the weather permits – i.e. if it's hot, dry and sunny with a good flow of air – the biltong can be fully dried outside (see p.103).

Store the biltong wrapped in waxed paper. It will keep for 2–3 weeks if semi-dried and for up to 2 years when fully dried.

Bresaola

TECHNIQUES	Dry-curing, wet-curing, air-drying
CURING TIME	Minimum 19 days

This recipe is adapted from *The River Cottage Meat Book* and is a truly wonderful way to deal with a joint of beef that, to my mind, is all too often turned into an inferior roast. Beef that has been through this magical, aromatic, boozy baptism turns a deep purple on the outside, and thin slices of it – arranged on a platter and finished with a drizzle of olive oil – look like beautiful stained-glass windows.

The method starts off with a dredging of dry cure and then a good drenching in a cold red wine bath before air-drying.

Serves about 30 (a few slices each)

A joint of beef topside or silverside, about 4kg

For the cure

About 120g coarse sea salt (i.e. 3% of the weight of the beef)
12 sprigs of rosemary
12 bay leaves, torn
20 cloves
4 garlic cloves, peeled and crushed
1 tbsp black peppercorns, freshly cracked
2 tsp dried chilli flakes
5–6 strips of finely pared orange zest
5–6 strips of finely pared lemon zest
75cl bottle of red wine

Equipment

Food-standard container
Butcher's hooks and string

Trim the outside of the meat, removing any fat or sinews.

Mix together all the dry ingredients for the cure and place in a food-standard container into which the joint will fit quite snugly.

Add the meat, turning it to coat well. This way of applying the cure mix is often called 'dredging'. Cover and leave in a cool place – the fridge if you like – for 4 days, turning the meat every other day.

Pour over the bottle of wine, or at least enough wine to virtually cover the meat, and return to the fridge. Turn the meat once a day for 5 days, then remove it from the marinade and pat dry with a clean tea towel (though not one that carries any sentimental value as it will get badly stained).

Tie up the meat with string, using the butcher's knot (see pp.148–9), and hang it in a dry, cool and draughty place such as an outbuilding, covered porch or poorly made shed (see p.103) – or put it in the fridge – for at least 10 days, but closer to 3 weeks for a more traditional finish.

When ready, it should be fairly hard to the touch on the surface but the centre will be silky smooth and slightly giving. The bresaola might need to be trimmed of the hard discoloured exterior before slicing, especially if it has hung for a longer period. Slice it very thinly, across the grain of the meat, like a giant salami.

A finished bresaola can be hung in a cool place for up to a month and used as and when you need it. In warm or humid weather, transfer it to the fridge.

Lamb culatello

TECHNIQUES	Dry-curing/wet-curing hybrid, air-drying
CURING TIME	Minimum 5 months

I have taken some liberties with this method but it is with the best intentions. The term culatello traditionally refers to the boned back half of a pig's hind leg that has been sewn up in a pig's bladder and cured for up to 4 years. My version uses the same set of muscles from a boned leg of lamb but does away with the bladder, replacing it with an ox bung casing. It came about as a result of my attempts to find a good way to cure a leg of lamb. Ready to eat within just 5–6 months, the recipe is a great example of how you can apply a traditional method in a new way to create something different but, to my mind, of equal excellence.

Makes 1 culatello (serves about 10)

1 ox bung casing
1 boned, skinned and rolled rump of halved lamb leg (the largest muscle from the rear top part of the leg, shank removed), about 1–2kg

For the cure
About 30–60g PDV salt (i.e. 3% of the weight of the lamb)
1 tsp chopped rosemary
½ tsp chopped thyme
½ glass of red wine

Equipment
Ziplock food bag
Butcher's hooks and string

Soak the ox bung casing overnight in cold water.

Put the piece of lamb into a ziplock food bag.

For the cure, mix the salt with the herbs and add to the bag, then pour in the red wine. Seal the bag and place on a tray or other container so that the liquid doesn't spill, should it leak from the bag. Refrigerate for 1 day per kg of lamb.

After the allotted time, remove the lamb from the bag, rinse and pat dry. Place the lamb in the ox bung. This might at first be a tight squeeze but eventually it should fit. Tie the length of the encased lamb using the butcher's knot (see pp.148–9).

Air-dry the cured lamb (see p.103) for 5 months or until it's lost 30% of its original weight. It will be dry throughout but with a tender texture. Thinly slice to serve.

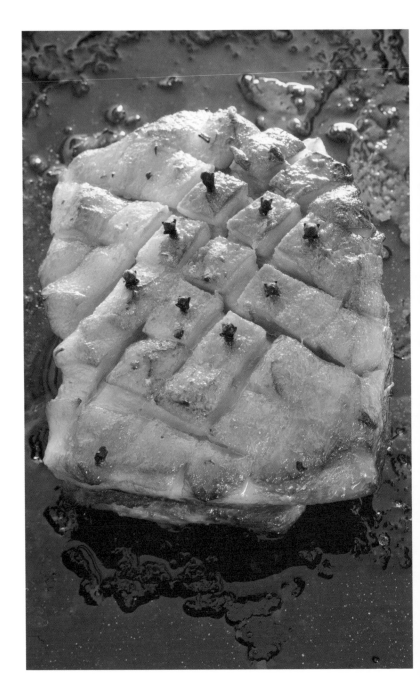

Cider-cured ham

TECHNIQUES	Wet-curing, air-drying, cold-smoking (optional)
CURING TIME	Minimum 15 days

There are few better partnerships than pork and apple. There are even fewer better than pork and cider, a bit of old English alchemy. This recipe can be applied to a whole leg of pork, weighing 10kg or more, but you can use a smaller portion off the bone, as I prefer to do, or even a chump. The quantities here are for a small, whole boned-out leg or half a large leg. For a large leg from a mature baconer on the bone, you may need to double the quantities and invest in a huge stockpot.

Serves 6–8

A whole or ½ leg of free-range
    pork, boned and chilled

For the brine
1.1kg PDV salt
1 litre pressed apple juice
    (i.e. not from concentrate)
1 litre strong dry cider
2.5 litres water
1kg demerara sugar
1kg dark brown sugar or black treacle
20–30 juniper berries
30g black peppercorns, crushed
10 bay leaves, crushed
10 cloves

Equipment
Food-standard brine tub
Food-standard tray
Cold smoker (optional)

Put all the ingredients for the brine into a large saucepan, bring to the boil and leave to cool. Transfer to a food-standard brine tub and chill to 3–4°C.

Weigh your piece of pork, then place it in the tub and submerge it completely in the brine, using a food-standard tray with a weight on top. Leave the pork in the brine, in the coolest place you can find if the tub is too large for your fridge, for a minimum of 3 days (or maximum of 4 days) for every kg. The minimum time will suffice if you plan to cook and eat the ham soon after it has finished curing, but you should use the maximum time if you intend to keep it much longer.

After its allotted time, remove the ham from the cure, wipe it dry with a cotton cloth and hang it to dry in a well-ventilated cool place for 24 hours.

You can then cold-smoke it if you like: hang it high above a hardwood fire or put it in your cold smoker and either smoke it continuously for 24 hours or intermittently (6–12 hours a day) for 2–4 days. The ideal air temperature where the ham is smoking is 27°C; a little variation won't hurt, but it should not exceed 40°C.

Smoked or unsmoked, this ham keeps well if you go for the maximum cure time: hang it in a well-ventilated outbuilding, or covered porch where a draught can get to it but the rain can't (see p.103), and it should keep right through the winter months. In warmer weather, hams are at risk from flies and other bugs, so it's best to get them cooked before too long. A minimum-cure-time unsmoked ham should be kept in the fridge, wrapped in a cloth or muslin, but not plastic, and cooked within a month of curing.

Cooking your ham

I've read a lot of recipes that suggest hams should be soaked in plenty of fresh water, which is changed every 12 hours, for 24–48 hours depending on the length of the cure, before boiling. I don't subscribe to this – it smacks of not getting the original cure right. If you draw the moisture out and drive the salty cure in, then undo part of this by soaking it in water, the ham won't know whether it's coming or going.

Instead, put your ham in a large cooking pot, cover with water, bring to the boil and simmer very gently for 2–5 hours, depending on size. If the water tastes very salty after the first hour of cooking, pour at least half of it away and top up with fresh boiling water from the kettle. When the fat starts to separate from the meat, it should be ready.

You can either serve the ham plain-boiled (I love it as a pared-down meal with plain boiled spuds and a dollop of mustard) or add a further stage of baking, which is what I tend to do when I serve it as a festive centrepiece on Boxing Day: remove the ham from the cooking liquor and allow it to cool slightly. Preheat the oven to 180°C/Gas mark 4. Slice the skin off the ham and score the fat in a diamond pattern. Mix 100g honey with 2 tbsp English mustard to make a honey mustard glaze and smear it over the ham. Place in the oven for about 40 minutes–1 hour, depending on size, until caramelised. Serve hot or at room temperature. Sumptuous.

Note: There is an alternative method for brining, using a brine pump. Instead of submerging the product in the brine you use a pump to inject the brine into the product. I find this method too hit or miss as it doesn't give a uniform result. And it doesn't work at all on anything smaller than a large chicken.

Pressed ox tongue

TECHNIQUE	Wet-curing
CURING TIME	Minimum 3 days

Often mistaken for an organ and categorised as offal, tongue is in fact a muscle. It may not currently be on your top-ten ingredients list but, with a little effort, this cut of meat can be transformed into something tasty for the whole family.

Serves 10

1 ox tongue

For the brine
2 litres water
500g salt
1 tsp dried red chilli flakes
1 clove
2 bay leaves
½ tsp white peppercorns

Equipment
Food-standard brine tub

Put all the ingredients for the brine into a large saucepan and stir well. Place over a low heat until the salt is fully dissolved, then bring to the boil and let bubble for 1–2 minutes. Remove from the heat and allow to cool completely.

Place the tongue in a food-standard brine tub, such as a large plastic box, and cover completely with the brine. Weigh the tongue down with a weight placed on a tray or plate so that it is fully submerged. Leave in a cool place for 1 day per kg.

Remove the tongue from the brine and rinse thoroughly in cold water. Put it into a saucepan and cover with fresh cold water. Bring to a simmer and cook gently for 3–4 hours until the tongue is really tender. Allow it to cool slightly in the liquor.

When the tongue is cool enough to handle, lift it out of the pan and peel away the coarse skin. Put the tongue into a basin or terrine in which it fits quite snugly. Pour on a little of the cooking liquor (which will set like a jelly as it chills). Place a small plate on top of the tongue and put a heavy weight on top. Allow it to cool completely and then refrigerate for 2 days.

Turn the pressed tongue out of the bowl (it may be necessary to immerse the bowl in warm water to release the tongue). Serve it thinly sliced, with assorted pickles.

Salt beef

TECHNIQUE	Wet-curing
CURING TIME	Minimum 2 days

This classic method for making delicious open-textured salt beef is adapted from *The River Cottage Meat Book*. You can also use it to cook an ox tongue. Conventional wisdom has it that the best cuts for salt beef are silverside and brisket, the former being much superior. I have experimented with various cuts, including foreflank and even a large chunk of shin on the bone. They all work well but in my book the fattiest, cheapest cuts give the most open-grained texture, which is what I like. So I stick to brisket and foreflank for this recipe – both usually on the bone. I tend to keep the leaner silverside for the Italian dry-cured beef, bresaola.

Serves 10 or more

2–3kg piece of beef brisket or foreflank
  (or use a whole ox tongue)

For the brine
5 litres water
1kg PDV salt
600g demerara or light brown sugar
1 tsp black peppercorns
1 tsp juniper berries
5 cloves
4 bay leaves
A sprig of thyme

To cook the beef
1 bouquet garni
1 carrot, peeled and chopped
1 onion, peeled and chopped
1 celery stick, chopped
1 leek, washed and chopped
½ garlic bulb (sliced horizontally
  to cut through the cloves)

Equipment
Food-standard brine tub
Food-standard tray

Put all the ingredients for the brine into a large saucepan and place over a low heat, stirring occasionally until the salt and sugar have fully dissolved. Bring to the boil and allow to bubble for 1–2 minutes, then remove from the heat and leave the brine to cool completely.

Put your chosen piece of beef into a food-standard brine tub and cover it completely with the brine. Weigh the meat down if necessary with a weight placed on a tray or a piece of wood to keep it submerged.

Leave the piece of beef to cure in a cool place for 1 day per kg, then remove it from the brine.

To cook the beef, put it into a saucepan with the bouquet garni, vegetables and garlic. Cover with fresh water and bring to a gentle simmer. Poach it very gently on the hob or in the oven (preheated to 150°C/Gas mark 2) if you prefer. Cook until the meat is completely tender and yielding when pierced with a skewer. A 3kg piece of beef will take 2½–3 hours.

Serve the hot salt beef carved into fairly thick slices, with lentils, beans or boiled potatoes and either creamed fresh horseradish or good English mustard. Alternatively, you can serve it cold. It will keep for a further week in prime condition; thereafter it will begin to dry out too much.

Note: If you've cured an ox tongue rather than a piece of beef, you will need to peel off the coarse skin before serving.

Beer-brined smoked ox heart

TECHNIQUE	Wet-curing
CURING TIME	Minimum 24 hours

My mum used to cook a stuffed ox heart, which was amazing. The closest thing I've had to it was made in the River Cottage kitchen by sous chef Andy Tyrell. I've combined elements of both dishes here, which hopefully does them proud.

Serves 4–6

1 ox heart, trimmed of all excess fat
    and connective tissue

For the brine

1.5 litres dark beer or stout
180g PDV salt
250g dark brown sugar
50g demerara sugar
5 bay leaves
2 star anise
1 cinnamon stick

For the stuffing

250g bacon offcuts, finely diced
1 small onion, peeled and finely diced
1–2 garlic cloves, peeled and crushed
50g fresh breadcrumbs
2 tbsp finely chopped sage
A good pinch of freshly grated nutmeg
Salt and freshly ground black pepper

To cook the beef

1 tbsp beef dripping (or olive oil)
2 onions, peeled and sliced
4–5 carrots, peeled
1–2 garlic cloves, peeled and chopped

For the brine, set aside 500ml of the beer (for the stuffing and cooking), then put the remaining 1 litre in a stockpot with all the other brine ingredients. Bring to the boil, stirring to dissolve the salt and sugar. Allow the brine to cool right down and refrigerate it. Place the ox heart in the brine and leave in the fridge for 24 hours.

For the stuffing, mix all the ingredients in a bowl, with a small glass of the reserved beer, until well combined. Slice the heart horizontally to give large, more or less rectangular pieces. In each, put a teaspoonful or two of the stuffing mix. Roll up to make large 'hearty' parcels and secure with wooden skewers to hold the stuffing in.

To cook, heat the dripping or oil in a cooking pot over a medium heat and fry the onions, whole carrots and garlic until well coloured, then add the rest of the held-back beer. Cook gently, either on the hob or in the oven (preheated to 170°C/Gas mark 3), for 2½–3 hours until tender and giving. Serve hot, with creamy mash.

Brined Christmas turkey

TECHNIQUE	Wet-curing
CURING TIME	Minimum 24 hours

I have never been a big fan of roast turkey. It is such a difficult thing to get right, what with the size, its tendency to dry out and the bands of sinew and tendon in the legs. The solution is to brine your turkey first, then it will remain moist and take on extra flavour. This is loosely based on a traditional American Thanksgiving recipe (leaving out the usual practice of deep-frying the brined bird before serving).

Serves 6–8

1 free-range turkey, 4.5–5.5kg

For the brine
25 litres water
2.5kg PDV salt
500g demerara sugar
60g black peppercorns, cracked
2 heads of garlic, halved horizontally
2 onions, peeled and sliced

A bunch of tarragon (with stalks)
A bunch of parsley (with stalks)
5 bay leaves
4 lemons, halved
75cl dry vermouth or gin (optional)

Equipment
Large food-standard brine tub
Meat temperature probe

Place all the ingredients for the brine, including the herbs, lemon halves and vermouth, if using, in a stockpot and bring to the boil, stirring often, to encourage the salt and sugar to dissolve. Remove from the heat and allow to cool completely; leave overnight if possible.

Put the turkey into a food-standard brine tub, pour on the brine and place a plate or something similar on top to keep the turkey submerged. If you can get the tub in your fridge, do so. If not, put it in a cool place, such as a pantry. Keep your turkey in the brine for 24–36 hours. Remove the turkey from the brine, rinse it well under cold water, then pat dry. Let it rest, uncovered, in the fridge for at least 3 hours.

Cook the turkey as per your instructions. Alternatively, preheat the oven to 220°C/Gas mark 7 and roast the turkey for 40 minutes (this initial blast is to get the heat right into the bird), then lower the oven setting to 170°C/Gas mark 3 and cook for a further 3½ hours or until the internal temperature reaches 70°C. Check by placing a meat temperature probe in the thickest part of a thigh. To be fancy, you could cure some of your own bacon and wrap the turkey breast in it.

Duck confit

TECHNIQUES	Dry-curing, confit
CURING TIME	Minimum 3 days

Normally curing relies on large quantities of salt; any fat present in the meat aids the curing process and enhances the flavour of the finished product. Here, the balance is tipped in the opposite direction. A large quantity of fat is used first to slowly cook the meat, creating a unique succulent texture, then as a preservative, forming a protective seal that stops oxygen and light spoiling the meat.

Salt is used too, but in the form of a very light cure that seasons more than it preserves. The preserved duck can be stored in the fridge for 6 months or more. When required, it is freed from its suspended animation in the solid fat, and given a quick, hot blast of cooking that crisps the skin.

The best and most cost-effective way of making duck confit is to buy a whole duck. You can retrieve the fat from the carcass, then joint the bird, using the legs for confit. The breasts can be hot-smoked (see p.226) or dry-cured (see p.183) and the rest of the carcass can be roasted and used to make stock.

There should be enough fat on the duck, when rendered down, to cover both legs. If you don't want to buy a whole bird or there isn't enough fat you can buy a carton of duck fat. Confit fat can be used several times until it becomes too salty.

Serves 2

1 large, whole duck (see above)
OR
2 duck legs, about 200g each, plus 450g duck fat, lard or a mixture of both (see above)

For the cure
About 200g PDV salt (to cover the duck legs liberally)
A few sprigs of thyme, lightly bruised (optional)
20g black peppercorns, cracked (optional)

Equipment
Food-standard tray

If you are rendering the fat from a whole duck yourself, first pull all the fat away from the body, then joint the duck. Put the fat into a heavy-based saucepan with about 50ml water and place over a very low heat. Leave it, uncovered, for several hours until the fat has rendered down to a clear liquid.

Pass the liquid fat through a fine sieve into a bowl to remove any impurities. Place the duck legs on a food-standard tray.

Mix together the ingredients for the cure. This recipe requires a significant quantity of salt, equivalent to covering both of the duck legs. If you would like to store the legs in fat for anything more than a week, this amount will make the preservation more stable. Cover the duck legs all over with the cure and refrigerate overnight.

The following day, wash off the cure and pat the duck legs thoroughly dry, using a clean tea towel.

Preheat the oven to its lowest setting. Gently heat the fat you are using in a stockpot until it is liquid. Place the duck legs in the rendered fat, making sure they are completely covered. Put the stockpot over a medium heat on the hob. As soon as the fat begins to simmer, transfer the stockpot to the low oven and leave the duck legs to confit slowly: they will take between 8 and 10 hours to cook. When ready, they should be tender and submerged in clear fat. If you intend to cook the duck legs within a week, keep them in the stockpot and allow the fat to cool and set in the fridge.

If you want to store the duck legs for longer, transfer them to a container such as a sterilised Kilner jar or earthenware pot. Pour the warm, liquid fat from the stockpot over them so they are completely submerged. Allow to cool, then cover with cling film before putting on the lid and refrigerating. Light can turn the fat rancid, so wrap the jar in foil to block it out completely. Leave the legs to mature for up to 6 months in the fridge. Their flavour will improve all the while.

To cook the legs, take the container from the fridge and leave it at room temperature for several hours to allow the fat to soften. Preheat the oven to 200°C/Gas mark 6. Remove the duck legs from the fat and place them in a roasting tin. Roast in the oven for 20 minutes, or until the skin is crisp.

Sauerkraut

TECHNIQUES	Brining, fermentation
CURING TIME	2 weeks

This is a really simple brining and fermentation method for cabbage, giving it a tangy, bright lift while maintaining its fresh texture. Sauerkraut can be eaten raw, but it also benefits from being braised in a light stock, which reduces the acidity levels but none of the flavour. Cooked like this, it goes particularly well with the smoked ham hock terrine on p.239. When brining vegetables, a 6% salt to liquid ratio is perfect (see p.112). Sauerkraut is a really great probiotic food.

Serves 10

1 red or green cabbage, about 1kg,
   thinly sliced or shredded

Equipment
Kilner jar or large preserving jar(s)

For the brine
1 litre water
60g PDV salt

For the brine, put the water and salt in a cooking pot and bring to a simmer, stirring occasionally to encourage the salt to dissolve. Allow to cool, then chill the brine in the fridge to about 5°C.

Put the shredded cabbage into a bowl or plastic container and pour in the chilled brine so that it covers the cabbage. It is quite tricky to keep cabbage submerged in brine, but placing a sieve, the right way up, on top of the cabbage, works well.

Cover the bowl (with the sieve still on top) with a tea towel or cling film and leave in a cool place, such as a pantry, with an ambient temperature no higher than 23°C, for 2 weeks. This will allow fermentation to begin without letting harmful bacteria multiply.

After 2 weeks, drain the brine from the cabbage. Your sauerkraut is now ready to eat. You can either serve it as it is, in a similar fashion to coleslaw, or place it in a pan, cover it with chicken stock and simmer it very gently for 30 minutes or so.

You can store the sauerkraut in a sealed Kilner jar or large jars in the fridge for up to 3 weeks.

Hot-smoked mackerel

TECHNIQUES	Dry-curing, hot-smoking
CURING & SMOKING TIME	16 minutes

I am fortunate to live and work within casting distance of Lyme Bay. When the mackerel are running, we clock off work with our fishing rods in hand and head off down to the shoreline. Our first job is to set a small driftwood fire going on the pebbled beach and then it is time to tie feathers and a small ledger on the end of our lines, cast them out into the rushing waves and spin them back to shore. It's a wonderful place to be if you don't catch a fish – and even better if you do.

Hot-smoking mackerel fillets fresh from the sea is one of my favourite things to do. Lightly salted and cooked over oak sawdust, these are fantastic. They can also be used to make a tasty pâté – a great way to deal with a glut of shimmering fish.

Serves 4

4 mackerel, filleted and pin-boned

For the cure
A generous pinch of sea salt per fillet
30g dill, finely chopped (optional)

For smoking
Oak wood chips

Equipment
Kitchen tweezers
Hot smoker

Check the mackerel fillets for pin bones and remove with tweezers. Add a pinch of the cure to the flesh side of each mackerel fillet (or just splash with sea water). After 8 minutes wash off the cure (with sea water if you're on the beach) and pat dry. If you've used sea water to start with, just pat the fish dry.

Prepare the hot smoker with the oak wood chips (see pp.118–22), place on the fire or other heat source and smoke the mackerel fillets for 8 minutes. Eat immediately.

Hot-smoked mackerel pâté

Skin 250g hot-smoked mackerel fillet and put half in a food processor with 2 tsp freshly grated horseradish, 1 tbsp crème fraîche, 1 tsp caster sugar and 1 tbsp lemon juice. Blend until smooth, then transfer to a bowl. Flake the remaining fish and stir through the pâté with 1 tsp coarsely ground black pepper and a handful of dill or chives, finely chopped. Taste for seasoning and add more lemon juice, if necessary. Serve the pâté on buttered rye bread.

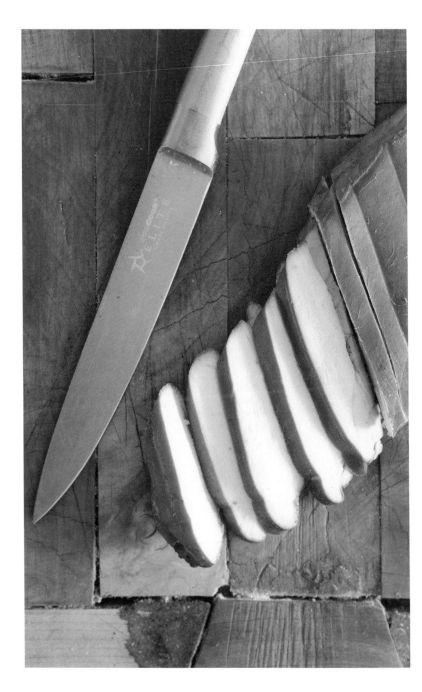

Hot-smoked chicken
or pheasant breasts

TECHNIQUES	Dry-curing, hot-smoking
CURING & SMOKING TIME	32–35 minutes

This quick and easy recipe is a brilliant way to add flavour to poultry and game and it keeps the meat lovely and moist. I have used the same cure on rabbit loins with great success.

Serves 4

4 organic chicken or pheasant breasts, skinned and boned

For the cure
150g demerara sugar
150g PDV salt
1 tsp juniper berries, bruised
4 bay leaves, shredded
1 tsp black peppercorns, coarsely crushed

For smoking
Oak (or other) wood chips

Equipment
Food-standard tray
Hot smoker

Mix all the cure ingredients together in a bowl.

Take a small plastic food-standard tray or something similar that is large enough to hold the chicken or pheasant breasts in a single layer. Scatter half the cure over the base of the tray, lay the chicken breasts on the mixture and scatter the remaining cure over the top of them.

Allow the meat to cure for just 12–15 minutes, then rinse the cure from the meat under a cold running tap and dry thoroughly with a tea towel. Store overnight in the fridge if you do not want to use them straight away.

Prepare the hot smoker with the wood chips (see pp.118–22), place on your heat source and hot-smoke the chicken breasts over a gentle heat for 20 minutes or until they are cooked through. Allow to rest for 5 minutes before serving.

Smoked chicken (or pheasant) is delicious served cold with chutney, salad and good bread.

Hot-smoked rose-cured beef
with wood sorrel

TECHNIQUES	Dry-curing, hot-smoking
CURING & SMOKING TIME	Minimum 14 hours

There are times when it feels all the stars are aligned and everything is magically in place. The birth of this dish was one of them. Rarely have I been part of a food event as unique and stellar as the MAD Symposium in Denmark, inaugurated by René Redzepi, head chef of Noma. As part of this amazing trip, Hugh, Gill Meller and I had the opportunity to cook for some of the best chefs in the world (including Ferran Adrià and Fergus Henderson, as well as René himself). With the help of some fantastic ingredients, Gill's confidence and Hugh's direction and competitive edge, we put together one of the most memorable dishes I have ever been party to. This is a version of that dish. Do try it.

Serves 4

1kg piece of aged beef sirloin,
   boned and trimmed

For the cure
200g fragrant rose petals
50g caster sugar
200g coarse sea salt
1 tsp black peppercorns, coarsely
   crushed

For the dressing
100g caster sugar
100ml water
100g small alpine strawberries
   (or sliced standard strawberries)
100g wild wood sorrel
   (or common sorrel)

For smoking
Oak wood chips

Equipment
Food-standard tray
Hot smoker

Trim the sirloin of any extraneous fat. Put all of the cure ingredients into a bowl and mix together thoroughly, making sure you bruise the rose petals so they release their fragrance.

Take a plastic food-standard tray or something similar, large enough to hold the piece of beef. Scatter half the cure over the base of the tray, lay the sirloin on the mixture and scatter the remaining cure over the top. Cover the tray and leave the meat to cure in a cool place for 1½–2 hours.

Rinse the cure off the beef under a cold running tap, then allow it to dry thoroughly – ideally overnight covered in the fridge.

Meanwhile, for the dressing, put the sugar, water and strawberries in a pan over a low heat and cook gently for about 5 minutes until the berries have released their juices and you have a syrup. Let this cool, then strain and chill it.

Prepare the hot smoker with the wood chips (see pp.118–22), place on your heat source and hot-smoke the sirloin for 30 minutes or until it is cooked to your liking. If you prefer, after 15 minutes, you can remove it from the smoker and sear it on a hot griddle or barbecue (as we did in Denmark). This will give it a lighter smoke but with a caramelised thin crust. Allow the beef to rest for 5 minutes.

Thinly slice the cured beef on to a platter. Dress it with the strawberry syrup and garnish liberally with the wood sorrel. Serve to the great and the good – with a strong hint of pride.

Hot-smoked pork tenderloin

TECHNIQUES	Dry-curing, hot-smoking
CURING & SMOKING TIME	Minimum 1¼ hours

When we get a whole pig carcass in the kitchen at River Cottage, the tenderloin is generally one of the first cuts we deal with. It does not lend itself to being frozen because it is so lean. Instead, we often whip it out, before any other major butchery takes place, dry-cure it and get it in the hot smoker.

Serves 4–6

1 free-range pork tenderloin

For the cure

200g demerara sugar
200g PDV salt
5 bay leaves, shredded
20 juniper berries, bruised

For smoking
Oak wood chips

Equipment
Food-standard tray
Hot smoker

Using a sharp knife, trim the tenderloin of any fat and silvery sinew.

Mix all the cure ingredients together thoroughly in a bowl. Use the salt-box method (see p.98) to apply the cure to the tenderloin: place a handful of the cure in a small food-standard tray, sit the tenderloin on top and completely cover with another handful of the cure. Now, either cover with a clean tea towel or place in the fridge for an hour, by which time the meat will have lost some moisture, which will be apparent in the cure around it, and be firmer to the touch and slightly darker in colour.

Wash the cure from the tenderloin under a cold running tap and dry it thoroughly.

Prepare the hot smoker with the wood chips (see pp.118–22), place on your heat source and hot-smoke the tenderloin for 10–12 minutes. Allow to rest for 4 minutes.

At this point, you could finish off the tenderloin by frying it in a little butter, but I would only do that if you aren't sure the internal temperature of the meat has reached at least 65°C. We like to serve the tenderloin slightly pink in the middle – which we can do with confidence as the pork is of a high quality. It should be moist and melting with a golden-brown, smoky exterior. Slice and serve – it makes a delicious canapé.

Pine-smoked mussels
with spinach

TECHNIQUE	Hot-smoking
SMOKING TIME	5–8 minutes

Most of my favourite food experiences have been in the company of River Cottage pals, chief forager John Wright and head chef Gill Meller. Not only are they good company, they are also generous with their knowledge. They taught me this way to cook mussels, which derives from the French technique, *éclade de moules*. The spectacle equals the taste, the burning pine needles imparting a fantastic flavour.

Serves 4

2kg mussels
A knob of butter
1 tbsp olive oil
1 garlic clove, peeled and chopped
2 large handfuls of spinach
Sea salt and freshly ground black
    pepper

For smoking
A forager's basket full of very dry
    pine needles

Equipment
Kettle barbecue

Scrub the mussels well under a cold running tap and trim away the wiry beard from the side of the shell. Discard any mussels that are damaged or open (unless they close readily when you give them a sharp tap against the side of the sink).

Set a large metal tray outdoors supported on a flat surface, away from anything that could catch fire. It could be on a kettle barbecue or a bed of slate. Scatter a layer of pine needles over the tray. Lay the cleaned mussels hinge side up and side by side on top, then lay another stack of pine needles over the top, about 20cm high.

Set fire to the pine needles in several places, all upwind of the tray, and give them a good blow to get them going. Once the pine needles have completely burnt up (5–8 minutes) the mussels are ready to take out – carefully as the shells can be hot.

Place a pan over a medium heat and add the butter, olive oil and garlic. Cook for 1 minute, then add the spinach, cover and cook for 2–3 minutes until wilted. Add the pine-fired mussels in their shells, season with salt and pepper and heat through. It's important to cook mussels properly, especially if you've foraged them yourself, although the heat from the pine needles should have done the trick. Serve at once.

Hot-smoked oysters

TECHNIQUE	Hot-smoking
SMOKING TIME	2–3 minutes

Oysters are fabulous on their own – shucked out of their shells fresh and eaten raw. However, with a little bit of preparation and a light smoking, you can actually improve on the magic sensation of eating an oyster. Hot-smoked for only a few minutes, they retain their fresh texture and taste sweet, smoky and delicate. They are delicious just as they are, but I also love them with a little horseradish kick.

Serves 4 as a starter

12 oysters
2 tsp creamed horseradish (optional)

For smoking
Wood chips (of your choice)

Equipment
Kettle barbecue or hot smoker

Use either a kettle barbecue or hot smoker with your choice of wood chips (I like to use a combination of beech and ash). Have either the barbecue or smoker ready to place the wood chips in (see pp.118–22).

Shuck the oysters with an oyster knife, taking care not to lose any of the liquor from the shells. Carefully release the oysters without removing them from their shells. The oysters will have been partially cured from the salt in the liquor.

Pour off a small amount of the liquor from a couple of the rounded bottom shells into a bowl and reserve to add into the horseradish if using.

Put your wood chips into the embers of the barbecue or the hot smoker. Sit the oysters in their shells on the grill of the smoker or barbecue and put the lid on. Cook and smoke for 2–3 minutes. In the meantime, if you are using horseradish, mix it with the reserved liquor to loosen it and flavour it with a hint of the sea.

Lift out the oysters, using tongs as the shells will be quite hot, and place them, in their shells, on a serving board. Dab a little bit of horseradish on top of each one, if you wish. Serve straight away.

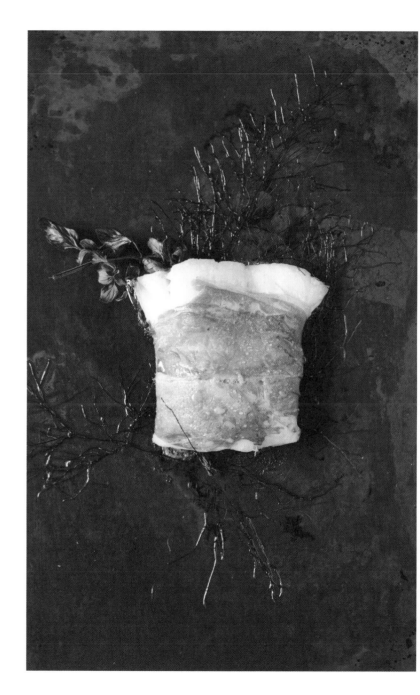

Smoked bream fillets
wrapped in prosciutto

TECHNIQUES	Dry-curing, hot-smoking
CURING & SMOKING TIME	25–30 minutes

Sea bass is often touted as being the best white fish to eat from our shores but my personal favourite is sea bream. For me, bream has a better flavour and firmer flesh, which smokes really well. It tastes even better if you happen to have caught it yourself. The combination of the bream fillet with a thin protective layer of aged prosciutto ham and smoke shows all the best attributes of curing and smoking on a plate. It has the immediacy of a fresh smoked fish coupled with the aged majesty of a home-cured ham and the textures are both melting and tender.

Serves 4

4 sea bream fillets, about 300g each
8 slices of prosciutto

For smoking
Wood chips (of your choice)

For the cure
250g demerara sugar
250g PDV salt
A bunch of chopped dill

Equipment
Food-standard tray
Barbecue or hot smoker

Have either the barbecue or hot smoker ready to place your chosen wood chips in (see pp.118–22). Mix all the cure ingredients together thoroughly in a bowl.

Put a small amount of the cure in a food-standard tray and place the bream fillets on top. Sprinkle more cure over the top of the fish so it has a liberal covering. Leave to cure in the fridge for just 15 minutes.

Rinse the fish under gently running cold water and then pat dry with a clean tea towel. Wrap the slices of prosciutto around the fish fillets. Put your wood chips into the embers of the barbecue or the hot smoker and smoke the wrapped bream fillets for 12 minutes or until cooked and lightly smoked. Serve with rye bread and salted butter and finish off with a splash of olive oil.

Variation
Other fish can be smoked in this way, such as pollack, salmon, gurnard or trout. You can also use small rosemary stems along with the wood chips for extra flavour.

Cedar-smoked duck breasts
with tea

TECHNIQUES	Dry-curing, barbecue hot-smoking
CURING & SMOKING TIME	40–45 minutes

I cook and smoke these duck breasts on the barbecue and that is where the cedar comes in. I call it 'wet barbecuing' not as a reference to a typical British summer, but because you soak the cedar plank in water before putting it into the hot barbecue to cook and smoke the duck. You will need a short, flat length of untreated wood or a small, non-precious chopping board made from cedar or oak (not a pine plank as this will create a bitter smoke), which fits inside your barbecue when the lid is on. You should soak this wood in water for a couple of hours prior to igniting the barbecue (or leave it out in a downpour!). If you don't have a length of cedar or other hardwood then you can still hot-smoke the duck using any combination of wood chips.

Serves 2

2 duck breasts with skin, about
    200g each

For the cure
250g demerara sugar
250g PDV salt
20g black peppercorns, freshly cracked
10 juniper berries

For smoking
Cedar plank or wood chips
    (of your choice)
A handful of loose black tea leaves,
    such as Earl Grey

Equipment
Food-standard tray
Kettle barbecue

Soak the cedar plank in cold water for 2 hours. Mix all the cure ingredients together thoroughly in a bowl.

Sprinkle a handful of the cure in a food-standard tray and place the duck breasts on top. Sprinkle another handful of cure over the duck so that it is gently dusted. Cover and leave to cure in the fridge for 30 minutes.

Heat up the barbecue. When it is ready (i.e. just as the coals are turning ash grey), place the sodden wooden board on top of the grill directly above the hot coals and put the lid on.

Rinse the duck breasts under a cold running water to remove any of the remaining partially dissolved cure, then pat them dry with a clean tea towel. During this time, the wooden board will begin to crackle and gently smoke.

Put a handful of normal everyday dry tea leaves into the embers of the barbecue. This will create more smoke with a sweet aroma. Now place the duck breasts on top of the wooden board and replace the lid so that the smoke created envelops the duck breasts while the heat of the board cooks them through. The lid will also act as an umbrella should it be raining.

After 10–15 minutes the duck breasts will be cooked to a nice, deep colour and flavoured with the exotic tea and wood smoke. They should also be wonderfully moist (but not in the way a picnic blanket gets any time between June and August). Serve the smoked duck breasts with a summer salad (dressed in a combination of rain mac, wellies and fingerless gloves).

Variation

Cedar-smoked Brie The cedar plank technique works really well for a whole Brie. You wouldn't normally hot-smoke cheese, but placing the cheese on the plank in the barbecue for 5 minutes makes it deliciously soft with a mild smoky taste.

Oak-smoked spiced lamb

TECHNIQUES	Marinade, barbecue hot-smoking
CURING & SMOKING TIME	Minimum 13 hours

If you own a kettle barbecue you'll be able to smoke and roast large joints of meat flavoured with a marinade or rub and the sweet smokiness from whichever wood combination you choose. For this recipe I rub a Merguez spice mix over a whole leg of lamb and let it infuse overnight before smoking the meat over charcoal.

Serves 6–8

A boneless leg of lamb, about 1.5kg,
   butterflied (flattened out)

For the rub
About 30g PDV salt (i.e. 2% of the
   weight of the lamb)
20g ground coriander
20g ground cumin
20g chilli powder
20g black peppercorns, freshly cracked
6 garlic cloves, peeled and chopped

For smoking
Wood chips (of your choice)

Equipment
Kettle barbecue

Mix together the ingredients for the rub and apply to the dried surface of the lamb leg with a gentle massage. Leave overnight.

The following day, light your barbecue and nestle a foil tray, three-quarters full of water, next to the coals (see p.129). Allow the coals to become grey and ashen as they get up to temperature. Remove the lamb from the fridge. The rub will have seasoned and salted the lamb so that it will take on the wonderful flavours of the spices as well as the smoke from the barbecue.

Lay the lamb on the grill above the coals and cook for 15 minutes.

Now move the lamb to the other side of the grill so that it is directly above the foil water tray. Put a handful of wood chips on the charcoal and place the lid, with the vent open, on top. Cook and smoke for 30 minutes. Check to see if the charcoal or wood needs replenishing, then replace the lid. Cook and smoke for a further 15 minutes, then remove. Rest the lamb for 10 minutes before slicing and serving.

Nduja
(Spreadable salami)

TECHNIQUES	Fermentation, cold-smoking, air-drying
CURING & SMOKING TIME	Minimum 8 days

This is a traditional recipe from the south of Italy. To call it salami is almost a misnomer – it ought really to be described as a young, partially cured, smoked, partially dried, fresh meat salami spread. Unlike normal salami, nduja is eaten only a week or so after making. Sliced out of its casing and spread on warm bruschetta, it's delicious.

Another difference from normal salami is that the meat tends to be belly of pork rather than shoulder, so it is a little fattier. You could let the nduja mature for 6–8 weeks to become fully dried salami but that would mean missing out on the unique texture of meat and fat cured in this way.

Makes 15–20 small nduja

Hog casings
2.5kg boneless free-range pork belly, trimmed of rind
50g PDV salt (i.e. 2% of the total weight of the meat)
200g smoked paprika (either hot or sweet)
50g cayenne pepper

For smoking
Oak (or other) wood chips or sawdust

Equipment
Meat mincer
Sausage stuffer
Butcher's hooks and string
Cold smoker

Soak the hog casings overnight in cold water.

Prepare the meat mincer and sausage stuffer as described on p.45. Mince the pork belly coarsely, using the 8mm plate.

Put the minced pork into a large bowl and add the salt and spices. Mix together thoroughly until evenly combined.

Pack the mixture into the barrel of the sausage stuffer and fit a medium nozzle on the end. Load the casings on to the nozzle and, once you have pushed any air through and can see the salami mix in the nozzle, tie the end with string following the method for tying salami, described and illustrated on pp.88–92. Fill the casing to create a 10–12cm sausage and tie the other end with string.

Continue to fill the casings until you have used all the mix. This should yield 15–20 small nduja salami.

Use a sausage pricker or sterilised needle to release any air bubbles so that the skin shrinks back against the meat. Leave the nduja salami to hang in a warm room at 26–29°C for 12–24 hours to allow the fermentation process to begin and help incubate the desired bacteria.

Once the sausages have rested overnight, fire up your cold smoker and cold-smoke the salami for 4 hours or so.

The salami should be air-dried for a week (see p.103). They are then ready to split, spread and eat. In the fridge, these salami will keep their moistness and spreadability for a further 4 weeks, but will dry out and firm up like a normal salami beyond that time.

Pastrami

This lovely American deli staple has a unique texture – quite dry, leaner than many cured meats, and with an almost flaky consistency. It's fantastic in sandwiches with pickles. The method takes in all the curing techniques: the beef is dry-cured, wet-cured, air-dried, then cold-smoked. Unsurprisingly, it's one of my favourite recipes!

Makes 30–40 generous slices

3kg joint of beef brisket or silverside

For the cure

60g PDV salt
6 garlic cloves, peeled and crushed
4 tbsp soft brown sugar
4 tbsp coarsely ground black pepper
1 tbsp ground ginger
2 tbsp coriander seeds, coarsely ground

For smoking

Oak (or other) wood chips or sawdust

Equipment

Food-standard tray
Butcher's hook
Cold smoker

Trim the meat of fat and put it into a large food-standard tray.

Mix the cure ingredients together and rub the mixture well into the meat. Cover and leave to cure in the fridge, allowing 1 day for every kg, turning the meat every day. As moisture is drawn from the meat, the dry salt will become a wet brine. After the allotted time, remove the meat, rinse and pat it dry with a clean tea towel.

Hang the meat in a cool, airy place for 5 days.

Now cold-smoke the meat at a temperature below 30°C for 6–8 hours. Remove from the smoker and leave hanging in a cool, dry place for 24 hours.

Put the smoked meat in a large pan, add enough water to just cover and bring to a simmer. Allow to simmer for 2–3 hours or until the meat is tender. Leave it to cool slightly in the liquid, then lift out. Put the meat into a dish, cover with a saucer and put a weight on top to press down. Refrigerate overnight before slicing. The pastrami will keep for 4–6 weeks in the fridge. It's fantastic in sandwiches with mustard and pickles.

Hunter's sausage

TECHNIQUES	Fermentation, cold-smoking, air-drying
CURING & SMOKING TIME	Minimum 4 weeks

This traditional German sausage was eaten as a snack on game shoots so it needed to fit in a pocket. Made using the salami method, pork and beef are minced through different plates for a rough and ready texture, and livened up with spices. You don't have to be in the wild, rifle in hand, to enjoy this sausage – it's great in any lunchbox.

Makes about 30 sausages

Hog casings
2kg boneless shoulder or hand
    of free-range pork
1kg chuck steak or beef skirt
60g PDV salt
1 tsp black peppercorns, freshly cracked
3 garlic cloves, peeled and minced
2 tsp mustard seeds, freshly ground
1 tsp garam masala
1 tsp ground ginger

For smoking
Oak (or other) wood chips or sawdust

Equipment
Meat mincer
Sausage stuffer
Cold smoker
Butcher's hooks and string

Soak the hog casings overnight in cold water.

Mince the pork and beef together through the large (8–10mm) mincer plate, so that the grain is coarse. Pass about one-third of the mixture through the mincer for a second time, using a smaller (6mm) plate. Combine the two different-textured meats with the salt, pepper, garlic and spices, using your hands or a wooden spoon.

Pack the mixture into the sausage stuffer and fit a medium (6mm) nozzle on the end. Load the hog casings on to the nozzle. Following the method for tying salami, described and illustrated on pp.88–92, tie one end with string, then fill the casing to a length of 15cm and tie the other end. Repeat to use all of the mixture.

Hang the sausages in a warm room (25–27°C), making sure they're not touching each other, for 12 hours to allow fermentation and incubation of the desired bacteria to happen. After this time, the surface of the sausage will be dry to the touch.

Fire up your cold smoker and smoke the sausages for 4–6 hours. Then hang them to air-dry in the correct conditions (see p.103). They should be ready in 4 weeks.

Pine-smoked Merguez

TECHNIQUE	Cold-smoking
CURING & SMOKING TIME	Minimum 20 hours

I love this spicy sausage, which combines two methods of dealing with lamb from very different origins. The classic, richly spiced Merguez mix comes from Morocco, but the tradition of pine-smoking lamb sausages can be traced to the French town of Morteau near the border with Switzerland, an area thick with spruce and pine forests. It's a winning combination. These Merguez are cooked, not eaten raw.

Makes 15–20 sausages

Sheep casings
1kg boneless lamb shoulder
18g PDV salt (for seasoning only)
2 garlic cloves, peeled and minced
1 tsp smoked paprika
1 tsp cayenne pepper
1 tsp black peppercorns, freshly cracked
½ tsp ground cumin
½ tsp ground allspice

For smoking
50/50 mix of pine and oak sawdust

Equipment
Meat mincer
Sausage stuffer
Cold smoker

Soak the sheep casings overnight in cold water.

Pass the lamb through the medium (6mm) plate of a mincer, then mix thoroughly in a bowl with all the remaining ingredients. Pack the mix into the sausage stuffer and fit the smallest nozzle on the end. Load the sheep casings on to the nozzle and begin to fill. Sheep casings are smaller and have a greater tendency to break than others, particularly if they dry out on the nozzle, or they're even slightly over-filled. To combat this, keep dowsing the loaded skins with cold water; any bagginess can be taken up by twisting them. Let the sausages dry naturally in the fridge overnight.

Put the pine and oak sawdust mix in the firebox of your cold smoker and smoke the sausages for 6–8 hours. They will now keep for 7 days in the fridge.

To cook the sausages, place in a cold frying pan and set over a moderate heat. They will release some of their lovely paprika-coloured and -flavoured fat, which becomes the cooking oil. The sausages will be cooked through and ready to eat in 20 minutes or so. Delicious served in flatbreads with a generous dollop of minted yoghurt.

Smoked ham hock terrine

TECHNIQUES	Wet-curing, air-drying, cold-smoking
CURING & SMOKING TIME	5–6 days

A smoked ham hock is often referred to as a knuckle and this recipe certainly packs a punch. A hock may be considered a lowly pork cut but it makes a fantastic terrine.

Serves 6–8

2 ham hocks, 1kg in total
A small bunch of flat-leaf parsley,
    leaves only, finely chopped

For the brine
3 litres cold water
1 litre pressed apple juice
1kg PDV salt
250g dark brown sugar
50g demerara sugar
5 bay leaves
2 star anise
1 cinnamon stick

For the stock
3 litres cold water
2 carrots, peeled
2 celery sticks
1 onion, peeled

For smoking
Oak (or other) wood chips or sawdust

Equipment
Food-standard brine tub
Butcher's hooks
Cold smoker

Put all the brine ingredients in a large pot and bring to the boil, stirring to dissolve the salt and sugar. Let cool, then transfer to a brine tub. Add the ham hocks, put a plate on top to keep them submerged and leave to cure in the fridge for 3 days (or the equivalent of 3 days per kg).

After the allotted time, remove the ham hocks and air-dry (see p.103) for 2 days.

Now fire up your cold smoker and cold-smoke the ham hocks for 4 hours.

Put the smoked hocks in a pan with the stock ingredients, bring to a simmer and simmer gently for 3 hours. Turn off the heat and leave to cool. Lift out the hocks. Remove and shred the meat, discarding the skin. Strain the stock into another pan and boil to reduce down. Line a terrine with cling film. Mix the shredded meat with the parsley, pack into the terrine and pour on enough of the reduced stock to cover.

Let the terrine cool, then refrigerate overnight or until set. Turn out on to a board and cut into thick slices. Serve with freshly baked bread and gherkins.

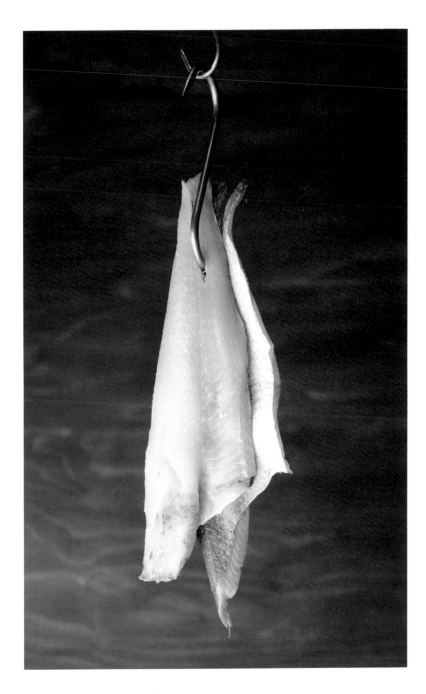

Cold-smoked pollack
with poached egg

TECHNIQUES	Dry curing, cold-smoking
CURING & SMOKING TIME	Minimum 6 hours

This simple recipe shows how a gentle lick of smoke across a wonderful fillet of fish can have an immense impact. It also reminds me of some of my favourite people – the Fisher family. Not just because we share the synchronicity of a surname that is related to our passions but because I know that Nick Fisher serves this dish to his wife Helen as an antidote to the stresses of the day, which just about sums up the practice of cold-smoking perfectly. If you have any left over, flakes of smoked pollack are lovely added to the smoked new potato salad on p.244.

Serves 2

2 pollack fillets, about 400g each

For the cure

75g PDV salt
75g light brown soft sugar
20g fennel seeds

To serve

A bay leaf
3–5 black peppercorns
500ml milk
2 tbsp cider vinegar
2 large very fresh organic eggs

For smoking

50/50 mix of beech and oak sawdust

Equipment

Food-standard tray
Cold smoker
Butcher's hooks

Mix all the cure ingredients together in a bowl and then sprinkle a couple of handfuls (or at least half of the mix) in a food-standard tray. Place the pollack fillets skin side down on the cure mix and then cover them liberally with the rest of the cure. Leave to cure in the fridge for at least 2 hours and no longer than 4 hours. (After this time the pollack flesh will lose its plump flakiness and become too dehydrated.)

After the allotted time, wash the residual cure from the fish under cold running water and then pat dry with a clean tea towel. Put the beech and oak sawdust in your firebox and either place your fillets on racks or hang them from butcher's hooks inside the smoking chamber. Occasionally, if you hang them like this, the fillets dry out around the hooks, causing the flesh to rip, and the fillets drop off the hook. Placing them flesh side down on a rack prevents this but you do sometimes get a cross-hatch pattern of the rack on the flesh which I don't actually mind. To avoid this you can tie string around the tail end of the fillet using a butcher's knot (see pp.148–9) and hang them up.

Depending on how smoky you like your pollack, you should cold-smoke it for anywhere from 4 to 8 hours.

After smoking, place the fillets in a saucepan in a single layer, cutting them in half to fit if necessary. Add the bay leaf and peppercorns and cover with the milk. Put the lid on and place over a medium heat until the liquid starts to simmer, then take off the heat. Leave covered for a couple of minutes to allow the fish to cook through in the residual heat.

Meanwhile, bring a small saucepan of water to the boil, add the vinegar and create a small whirlpool in the water by stirring with a spoon. Now carefully crack the eggs into the vortex. Turn the heat down to the minimum and cook the eggs for about 3 minutes. The whites should set around the central yolks like newly formed planets.

When the smoked pollack is cooked, remove it from the liquid and plate it up. Using a slotted spoon, remove the poached eggs from the pan, allowing any water to drain off, then place on top of the smoked pollack.

Oak-smoked Cheddar

TECHNIQUE	Cold-smoking
SMOKING TIME	Minimum 4 hours

I usually cold-smoke cheese as an extra product alongside something else, like a salami or side of bacon. It's incredibly simple and requires no curing or drying. You just slip your cheese into the cold smoker along with your other goodies and it will emerge, invitingly tanned and earthy, after its gentle, smoky immersion.

Hard cheeses, such as Cheddar, work best and absorb more flavour if their rind is first removed. Simply place a large piece of cheese, about 800g in weight, on a rack in the cold smoker for 4–6 hours and then enjoy. As with all cold-smoking, the temperature of the smoke chamber should not exceed 30°C. Spices or herbs can be added before smoking – try dusting Cheddar lightly with paprika.

You can experiment with smoking materials too. A traditional Danish cheese is smoked with fresh hay and nettles. The hay is lit, then damped down with nettles to create a thick smoke, which envelops the cheese. It is ready in about an hour.

Smoked new potato salad

TECHNIQUE	Cold-smoking
SMOKING TIME	Minimum 1 hour

I like to use new potatoes for this salad. As with anything you smoke, the surface must be dry before you put them in the smoker, or the smoke particles will only attach themselves to the moisture on the outside rather than creating a pellicle or smoky skin on the surface.

Serves 6–8

1kg new potatoes
1 red onion, finely chopped, or
    3 spring onions, sliced
A handful of herbs, such as snipped
    chives or young rosemary sprigs

For the vinaigrette
1 tsp coarse sea salt
1 garlic clove, peeled and chopped
2 tsp balsamic vinegar

For smoking
Oak (or other) wood chips or sawdust

Equipment
Cold smoker

Put the potatoes in a saucepan, add just enough water to cover them, bring to the boil and simmer for 15 minutes or until just tender. Drain them in a colander and allow them to cool and dry.

Remove the skin from the potatoes and place them in the cold smoker for just about an hour or so. Leave to cool.

For the vinaigrette, shake the ingredients together in a screw-top jar to emulsify. Taste and adjust the seasoning.

Toss the cold-smoked potatoes with the onion and the vinaigrette dressing. Scatter over the herbs to serve.

Variation

At the same time as cold-smoking the potatoes, you could place a few peeled, hard-boiled eggs in the cold smoker, then chop them and add to the salad. You could even cold-smoke the oil for the dressing to enhance the smoky effect.

Useful Things

Directory

Weschenfelder
www.weschenfelder.co.uk
A high-end, family-run, commercial supplier of kit, sundries, smokers, cures and casings. Also a wonderful reference resource for all things related to curing and smoking.

AW Smiths
www.awsmith.co.uk
A one-stop butcher's sundries website where you can buy all the kit you need to get curing.

Capreolus Fine Foods
www.capreolusfinefoods.co.uk
An award-winning, family-owned artisan smokehouse set in Rampisham, West Dorset, that specialises in the production of cured, air-dried and smoked meats and other charcuterie.

Denhay Farms Ltd
www.denhay.co.uk
A family-run farm producing award-winning, traditionally cured quality bacon and cheese.

Cabrito Goat Meat
www.cabritogoatmeat.co.uk
Supplier of good-quality goat meat.

Rusty Pig
www.rustypig.co.uk
A small, family-run business, based in rural Devon, who are experts in all things pig. Artisan producer with a specialist charcuterie shop/supper table.

Chesil Smokery
www.chesilsmokery.com
A commercial smokehouse using traditional artisan methods on ethical, sustainably sourced ingredients. Also runs an excellent online box scheme.

Monolith
www.monolith-grill.co.uk
Top-of-the-range barbecue and smoker equipment.

Salt Association
www.saltassociation.co.uk
A useful resource website with lots of information on edible salt.

www.rivercottage.net
The online home of River Cottage containing features, advice, forums and calendar of events.

@lamposts
Twitter account for Steven Lamb.

Acknowledgments

My role at River Cottage is varied and fun. It comes with some responsibilities. I teach, write, mess about in front of the camera and often find myself at serious gatherings around the world talking about what River Cottage stands for. Surrounded by experts and mavericks, I absorb everything like a sponge. I have been at River Cottage from the beginning. It has been the best apprenticeship possible and has afforded me the best job in the world. A job that has enabled me to find subjects I am passionate about and ultimately lead me to write this book. There are a few people I would like to sincerely thank for this:

Ray Smith was my teacher. Learning on the shoulder of Ray was such a wonderful experience. I hope this book proves I was a worthy student.

Hugh is a friend and an inspiration. Hugh, we do what we do on your behalf and in your name. What an amazing opportunity you have given us all.

I have worked with Rob Love longer than anyone I know, and he leads from the front with immense drive and vision.

Gill Meller is a legend. Most of my best food moments have had Gill at the centre of them. His team of chefs and KPs are second to none. Their support in putting the recipes together in this book has been immense.

Mark Diacono and John Wright share equal parts of humour, expertise and generosity of spirit. They have many books each under their belts but willingly gave advice and showed a genuine interest in helping me put this together.

Natalie Hunt and Xa Shaw Stewart at Bloomsbury are the dream team. A pleasure to work with, they add in a whole lot of guidance, direction, patience and fun. Thanks also to Marina Asenjo and Alison Glossop at Bloomsbury for their roles.

Nikki Duffy has been a tremendous asset. It is a pleasure to work with you, Nikki.

Gavin Kingcombe's photos are art. What a joy he is to collaborate with.

Janet Illsley has the eye of an eagle for detail and Will Webb's design is exemplary.

Chris Moorsby, Head of Butchery and Charcuterie at Leeds City College, and Peter R Sherratt of the Salt Association, thank you for your scientific checks.

My darling Elli, thanks for your love, support and encouragement, and for our two incredible little girls, Aggie and Betsy, who often sat on my lap whilst I was writing this book.

And, of course, thanks to my parents.

Index

Page numbers in italic refer to the illustrations

acetic acid 23
acidity: fermentation 105–7
  pH measures 54
additives, nitrates and nitrites 27, 30–5
Adrià, Ferran 216
ageing, controlled 26
air-drying 27, 103–4
  bresaola *102*, 190–1, *191*
  chorizo *170*, 171–3
  cider-cured ham *194*, 195–6
  cotechino *174*, 175–6, *177*
  goat violin 164–5, *165*
  guanciale 182–3, *183*
  hunter's sausage *234*, 235
  lamb culatello 192, *193*
  nduja (spreadable salami) *93*, 230–1, *231*
  pastrami *232*, 233
  prosciutto *12*, 156–9, *157*
  salami *166*, 167–8, *169*
  smoked ham hock terrine *238*, 239
  spalla and speck 184–7, *185*, *186*
  Szechuan-cured pork loin *68*, *69*, 178, *179*
  venison biltong 188–9, *189*
aitchbone, boning a leg of pork 74, 160
animal fats 25
animal welfare 25
antioxidants 20, 35
apple juice: cider-cured ham *194*, 195–6
ascetic acid 20

back bacon, dry-cured 142
back fat 81
backslopping 107–8
bacon 16
  back bacon 142
  cold-smoking *127*
  curing salts 31
  dry-cured streaky bacon 138–42, *140–1*
  dry-curing 96–8, 105
bacteria 20, 26–7
  backslopping 107
  fermentation 105–7
  nitrates and nitrites 30–2
  testing for 39
barbecues: cedar-smoked duck breasts 226–7, *227*
  charcoal 128, 129
  oak-smoked spiced lamb *228*, 229
  rubs and marinades 131–3
  smoking on 116–18, 128–31, 133
beef: beer-brined smoked ox heart *202*, 203
  bresaola *102*, 190–1, *191*
  cuts 76, *76*
  hot-smoked rose-cured beef 216–17, *217*
  hunter's sausage *234*, 235
  pastrami *232*, 233
  pressed ox tongue *198*, 199
  salt beef 200–1, *201*
beer-brined smoked ox heart *202*, 203
beetroot, gravadlax with 154, *155*
belly fat 81
belly of pork: boning 70, *71*, 72, *73*
  dry-cured streaky bacon 138–42, *140–1*
  rolled pancetta *144*, 145–8, *146*, *149*
biltong, venison 188–9, *189*
blowtorches 126
boning: air-dried ham 160–3, *161–2*
  belly of pork 70, *71*, 72, *73*
  hand of pork 62, *63*
  leg of pork 74, *75*
  loin of pork 68, *69*
  shoulder of pork 64, *65–7*
botulism 30–1, 32
boxes 50, *51*, 100
breadbins, as hot smokers *120*, 121
bream fillets, smoked *224*, 225
bresaola *102*, 190–1, *191*
Brie, cedar-smoked 227
brining 108–12, *109*, *113*
  brine bins 50
  brine injecting ham 196
  brine table 110
  brined Christmas turkey *204*, 205
  brines 111–12
  measuring salinity 52–4, 110–11
  pastrami *232*, 233
  sauerkraut *210*, 211
  smoked ham hock terrine *238*, 239
  wet-cure brines 26–7
brinometers 52–4, 110–11
butcher's blocks 50–2
butcher's hooks 52, *53*
butcher's saws 48–50, *49*
butcher's string 52, *53*
  tying pancetta 148, *149*
butter 25
buying meat 59

cabbage: sauerkraut *210*, 211
Cabrito 164
carcinogens, nitrates 32
casings 86, *87*
  filling and tying salami *88*, 89–93, *90–2*
caul fat 81
cedar-smoked duck breasts 226–7, *227*
cedar-smoked Brie 227
celery salt 32–5
charcoal: barbecues 128, 129

water smokers 131
charcuterie 16
Cheddar, oak-smoked 243, *243*
cheese
    oak-smoked Cheddar 243, *243*
    smoking 15, *79*, 116
chicken: brining 112
    hot-smoked chicken *214*, 215
cholesterol 25
chopping surfaces 37, 50–2
chorizo *170*, 171–3
    chorizo Scotch egg *172*, 173
cider-cured ham *194*, 195–6
citrus marinade 133
Clostridium botulinum 30
cloths, muslin 52, *53*, 103
cold-smoking 114
    cider-cured ham *194*, 195–6
    cold-smoked pollack *240*, 241–2
    equipment 114, 122–5, *123*
    fire/smoke management 126
    hunter's sausage *234*, 235
    nduja (spreadable salami) 93, 230–1, *231*
    oak-smoked Cheddar 243, *243*
    on open fires 122
    pastrami *232*, 233
    pine-smoked Merguez 236, *237*
    smoked ham hock terrine *238*, 239
    smoked new potato salad *244*, 245
    spalla and speck 184–7, *185*, *186*
Colonatta 151
colour, cured meats 31
commercial considerations 36–9
confit, duck *206*, 207–8, *209*
coppa 152–3
    salt-box method 98–100
cotechino *174*, 175–6, *177*
culatello, lamb 192, *193*
cultures, moulds 29
Cure #1 30, 32, 83
Cure #2 31, 83
curing: before smoking 114–16
    fermentation 105–8
    history 14–16
    salt 22–3
    science of 20
    traditional cured foods 16–17
    se also air-drying; dry-curing; wet-curing
curing salts 30–1

damp weather, and cold-smoking 126
demerara sugar 83
dry-curing 96–105, *97*
    air-drying 103–4
    back bacon 142
    basic method 98

bresaola *102*, 190–1, *191*
cedar-smoked duck breasts 226–7, *227*
cold-smoked pollack *240*, 241–2
coppa 152–3
dry-cured streaky bacon 138–42, *140–1*
duck confit *206*, 207–8, *209*
goat violin 164–5, *165*
gravadlax with beetroot 154, *155*
guanciale 182–3, *183*
hot-smoked chicken *214*, 215
hot-smoked mackerel *119*, 212, *213*
hot-smoked pork tenderloin 218, *219*
hot-smoked rose-cured beef 216–17, *217*
lamb culatello 192, *193*
lambcetta 147
lardo *150*, 151
pastrami *232*, 233
prosciutto *12*, 156–9, *157*
ratios 104–5
regulations 37–9
rolled pancetta *144*, 145–8, *146*, *149*
salt-box method 98–100, *99*
smoked bream fillets *224*, 225
spalla and speck 184–7, *185*, *186*
Szechuan-cured pork loin *68*, *69*, 178, *179*
total immersion method 100, *101*
venison biltong 188–9, *189*
duck 78
    brining 112
    cedar-smoked duck breasts 226–7, *227*
    duck confit *206*, 207–8, *209*
ducting, cold-smoking 124

eggs: chorizo Scotch egg *172*, 173
    cold-smoked pollack with poached egg *240*, 241–2
    smoked eggs 245
Environmental Health Office (EHO) 17, 36–7
enzymes 23
equipment 40–54
    accessories 48–52, *49*, *51*, *52*
    knives 48
    machinery 42–7, *43*, *44*, *46*
    measuring sundries 52–4
    smoking 114, *117*, 118–25, *120*, *123*
    sterilising 54
extraction fans 114
eye of meat, removing 64, 152

fat 23–5, *24*
    duck confit *206*, 207–8, *209*
    lamb fat 77
    lardo *68*, *150*, 151
    rancidity 29
    rendering *80*
    smoking and 20
    types of 81

fermentation 105–8
  chorizo *170*, 171–3
  cotechino *174*, 175–6, *177*
  hunter's sausage *234*, 235
  nduja (spreadable salami) 93, 230–1, *231*
  salami *166*, 167–8, *169*
  sauerkraut *210*, 211
filletto 178
fireboxes, cold-smoking 124
fires: barbecues 128–9
  cold-smoking on 116, 122
fish 78–9
  brining 112
  cold-smoked pollack *240*, 241–2
  gravadlax with beetroot 154, *155*
  hot-smoked mackerel *119*, 212, *213*
  smoked bream fillets *224*, 225
flare fat 81
Fleur de Sel 82
flies 103–4
food processors 45
Food Standards Agency (FSA) 17, 37
formaldehyde 20
freezers, regulations 37
fridges 104
frozen meat 59

game, cuts 78
garlic, smoking 116
gas, smoke-shacks 125
goat: cuts 78
  goat violin 164–5, *165*
gravadlax with beetroot 154, *155*
grinders 42–5, *43*
guanciale 182–3, *183*
  salt-box method 98–100

HACCPs (Hazard Analysis Critical Control Points)
  36–7, 39
halophiles 20, 26–7
ham: air-drying 103–4
  boning air-dried ham 160–3, *161–2*
  brine injection 196
  cider-cured ham *194*, 195–6
  cooking 196
  dry-curing 105
  pressing 163
  prosciutto *12*, 156–9, *157*
  smoked ham hock terrine *238*, 239
  total immersion method 100
hand of pork, skinning and boning 62, *63*
hay, smoking cheese 243
hearts: beer-brined smoked ox heart *202*, 203
  smoking *115*
herbs *84*, 85
  barbecue rubs 131–2

smoking 79, 118
Himalayan salt 30
history of curing and smoking 14–16
honey 83
hooks, butcher's 52, *53*
hot and sweet rub 132
hot-smoking 114
  cedar-smoked duck breasts 226–7, *227*
  equipment 114, *117*, 118–22, *120*
  hot-smoked chicken *214*, 215
  hot-smoked mackerel *119*, 212, *213*
  hot-smoked oysters *222*, 223
  hot-smoked pork tenderloin 218, *219*
  hot-smoked rose-cured beef 216–17, *217*
  oak-smoked spiced lamb *228*, 229
  pine-smoked mussels 220, *221*
  smoked bream fillets *224*, 225
humidity: air-drying 103, 104
  cold-smoking 126
  dry-curing 39
  hygrometers 39, 54
  and moulds 29
hunter's sausage *234*, 235
hydrometers 52–4, *53*
hygiene 27, 37, 133
hygrometers 39, 54

immersion method, dry-curing 100, *101*
inglenook fireplaces 116, 122
ingredients 56–93
'insta-cure' 30
intestines, casings 86
Inuit 14

jambon sacs 52, *53*, 103
Japanese seasonings 14

katsuobushi 14
kettle barbecues 128, 129, *130*
kiviaq 14
knives 48
knots, tying pancetta 148, *149*
kosher salt 83

labelling 39
lactic acid 20, 23, 31
lamb: cuts 77, *77*
  lamb culatello 192, *193*
  lamb violin 165
  lambcetta 147
  oak-smoked spiced lamb *228*, 229
  pine-smoked Merguez 236, *237*
lard 25
lardo 68, *150*, 151
laws 17, 36–9
leaf lard fat 81

leg of pork, boning 74, *75*
lignin 116
listeria 20
loin of pork, boning 68, *69*

machinery 42–7, *43*, *44*, *46*
mackerel 79
 hot-smoked mackerel *119*, 212, *213*
 hot-smoked mackerel pâté 212
MAD Symposium, Denmark (2012) 216
maggots 103–4
magnesium carbonate 82
malt vinegar 85
maple syrup 83
margarine 25
marinades, barbecue 131, 132–3
Maze fireboxes 114, 124, 125
measuring equipment 52–4
meat 59
 bacteria and 20
 brining 112
 buying 59
 mincers 42–5, *43*
 water content 26
 see also beef, pork *etc*
meat safes 52, 103
meat slicers *46*, 47
Merguez sausages 15
 pine-smoked Merguez 236, *237*
mincers 42–5, *43*
mortadella *11*, *180*, 181
moulds 20, 26, 27–9, *28*
muslin cloths 52, *53*, 103
mussels 79
 pine-smoked mussels 220, *221*
mustard marinade 133
mycotoxins 29
myoglobin 31

nduja (spreadable salami) 93, 230–1, *231*
nettles, smoking cheese 243
New Nordic Food Movement 17
nitrates 27, 30–5
nitric oxide 31
nitrites 27, 30–5
nitrosamines 31, 32
nitrosomyoglobin 31

oak-smoked Cheddar 243, *243*
oak-smoked spiced lamb *228*, 229
'off' flavours 29
oil, marinades 132–3
omega fatty acids 23
Organic Slow Food Movement 17, 35
ox heart: beer-brined smoked ox heart *202*, 203
 smoking *115*

ox tongue: pressed ox tongue *198*, 199
 salt beef 200–1
oxidation 29
oysters 79
 hot-smoked oysters *222*, 223

packaging 39
pancetta: boning belly of pork for 72, *73*
 dry-curing 105
 rolled pancetta *144*, 145–8, *146*, *149*
 tying 148, *149*
Parma ham: boning 160–3, *161–2*
 total immersion method 100
pastrami *232*, 233
pâté, hot-smoked mackerel 212
PDO (Protected Designation of Origin) status 17
PDV ('pure dried vacuum') salt *33*, *51*, 82–3
pellicle 116
Penicillium mould 20, 29
peptides 23
pH values 54
 and botulism 35
 fermentation 107
 measuring 54
 salt and 27
 smoking and 20
pheasant, hot-smoked 215
phenols 20, 116
pigs: breeds 156
 see also pork
pig's cheeks: guanciale 182–3, *183*
pine needles 116
 pine-smoked Merguez 236, *237*
 pine-smoked mussels 220, *221*
'pink salt' 30, 82, 83
piping, cold-smoking 124
planks, cedar 226–7
poaching, mortadella *180*, 181
pollack, cold-smoked *240*, 241–2
pork 59–75
 brining 112
 chorizo *170*, 171–3
 cider-cured ham *194*, 195–6
 coppa 152–3
 cotechino *174*, 175–6, *177*
 cuts *60*, 61
 guanciale 182–3, *183*
 hot-smoked pork tenderloin 218, *219*
 hunter's sausage *234*, 235
 lardo 68, *150*, 151
 mortadella *11*, *180*, 181
 nduja (spreadable salami) 93, 230–1, *231*
 prosciutto *12*, 156–9, *157*
 rolled pancetta *144*, 145–8, *146*, *149*
 salami *166*, 167–8, *169*
 skinning and boning 62–74, *63–75*

spalla and speck 184–7, *185*, *186*
Szechuan-cured pork loin 68, *69*, 178, *179*
  see also bacon
pork fat 25, 81
  lardo *150*, 151
potassium nitrate 31
potatoes: smoked new potato salad *244*, 245
poultry: brining 112
  see also chicken, duck *etc*
'Prague powders' 30, 83
pressed ox tongue *198*, 199
pressing ham 163
prosciutto *12*, 156–9, *157*
  boning 160–3, *161–2*
  dry-curing 105
  smoked bream fillets *224*, 225
  total immersion method 100
protein, effects of salt 23, 108
pumps, brine 196

Redzepi, René 216
regulations 17, 36–9
rendering fat *80*
rock salt 82
rose petals: hot-smoked rose-cured beef 216–17, *217*
rubs, barbecue 131–2

safety: hygiene 27, 37, 133
  meat slicers 47
salad, smoked new potato *244*, 245
salami *166*, 167–8, *169*
  backslopping 107–8
  bacteria 27
  casings 86, *87*
  curing salts 31–2, 35
  fermentation 105–7
  filling and tying *88*, 89–93, *90–2*
  moulds 29
  nduja (spreadable salami) 93, 230–1, *231*
  storing 93
salinometers 52–4, 110–11
salmon 79
  gravadlax with beetroot 154, *155*
salt *21*, 22–3
  barbecue rubs 131–2
  brining 108–12, *113*
  celery salt 32–5
  curing salts 30–1
  dry-curing 96–8, 104–5
  fermentation 105–7
  halophiles 20, 26–7
  measuring salinity 110–11
  PDV ('pure dried vacuum') salt *33*, *51*, 82–3
  reducing water content of meat 26
  rock salt 82
  salt-box method 98–100, *99*

sea salt 82, 83
  total immersion method 100, *101*
salt beef 200–1, *201*
saltpetre 31
salumi 16
saturated fats 25
sauerkraut *210*, 211
sausage fillers *44*, 45–7
sausages: casings 86, *87*
  chorizo *170*, 171–3
  cotechino *174*, 175–6, *177*
  hunter's sausage *234*, 235
  mortadella *11*, *180*, 181
  pine-smoked Merguez 236, *237*
sawdust 116, 118, 126
saws, butcher's 48–50, *49*
scientific principles 20
Scotch egg, chorizo *172*, 173
sea bream 79
  smoked bream fillets *224*, 225
sea salt 82, 83
sharpening knives 48
shellfish 79
  hot-smoked oysters *222*, 223
  pine-smoked mussels 220, *221*
shoulder of pork, boning 64, *65–7*
skinning hand of pork 62, *63*
Slow Food Movement 17, 35
smoke chambers 124–5
smoke generators 124
smoke-shacks 125
smoking 114–31
  on barbecues 128–31, 133
  cedar-smoked duck breasts 226–7, *227*
  cedar-smoked Brie 226
  cheese *15*, 79, 226, 243
  cider-cured ham *194*, 195–6
  cold-smoked pollack *240*, 241–2
  equipment 114, *117*, 118–25, *120*, *123*
  history 14–16
  hot-smoked chicken *214*, 215
  hot-smoked mackerel *119*, 212, *213*
  hot-smoked oysters *222*, 223
  hot-smoked pheasant 215
  hot-smoked pork tenderloin 218, *219*
  hot-smoked rose-cured beef 216–17, *217*
  hunter's sausage *234*, 235
  nduja (spreadable salami) 93, 230–1, *231*
  oak-smoked spiced lamb *228*, 229
  pastrami *232*, 233
  pine-smoked Merguez 236, *237*
  pine-smoked mussels 220, *221*
  science of 20
  smoked bream fillets *224*, 225
  smoked ham hock terrine *238*, 239
  smoked new potato salad *244*, 245

spalla and speck 184–7, *185*, *186*
vegetables 79, 116
water smokers 128–9, 131
wood 116–18
sodium ferrocyanide 535 82
Soil Association 32
spalla 184–7, *185*, *186*
speck 184–7, *185*, *186*
spices *84*, 85
  barbecue rubs 131–2
  smoking 79
starter cultures 27
  backslopping 107, 108
steak rub 132
steel, sharpening knives 48
sterilising equipment 54
storage, regulations 37
streaky bacon, dry-curing 138–42, *140–1*
string 52, *53*
  tying pancetta 148, *149*
sugar 27, 83
Szechuan-cured pork loin 68, *69*, 178, *179*

temperature: air-drying 103, 104
  barbecues 128
  cold-smoking 114, 122, 125
  hot-smoking 114, 121
  measuring 54
'Tender Mix' 31
tenderloin, hot-smoked pork 218, *219*
terrine, smoked ham hock *238*, 239
testing, laboratory 39
thermo-hygrometers 54
tikka marinade 132
tongue: pressed ox tongue *198*, 199
  salt beef 200–1, *201*
total immersion method, dry-curing 100, *101*
Trading Standards Office 17, 36–7
traditional cured foods 16–17
trans fats 25
trays 50
treacle 83
tubing, cold-smoking 124
turkey: brined Christmas turkey *204*, 205
  brining 112, *113*
tying pancetta 148, *149*
Tyrell, Andy 203

vegetables, smoking 79, 116
venison 78
  biltong 188–9, *189*
ventilation, smoking 114, 126
vinegar 85
  cleaning mould off 29
violina de capra 164

water, in meat 26
water smokers 128–9, 131
wet-curing 108–12, *109*
  and bacteria 26–7
  beer-brined smoked ox heart *202*, 203
  bresaola *102*, 190–1, *191*
  brined Christmas turkey *204*, 205
  brines 111–12
  cider-cured ham *194*, 195–6
  lamb culatello 192, *193*
  measuring salinity 110–11
  pressed ox tongue *198*, 199
  salt beef 200–1, *201*
  smoked ham hock terrine *238*, 239
  venison biltong 188–9, *189*
wine: bresaola *102*, 190–1, *191*
wood: charcoal 129
  and smoking 116–18
  wood 'papers' 116
working areas, regulations 37

yeasts 27

River Cottage Handbooks

River Cottage Handbook No.1

Mushrooms
by John Wright
introduced by Hugh Fearnley-Whittingstall

River Cottage Handbook No.2

Preserves
by Pam Corbin
introduced by Hugh Fearnley-Whittingstall

River Cottage Handbook No.3

Bread
by Daniel Stevens
introduced by Hugh Fearnley-Whittingstall

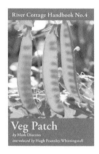

River Cottage Handbook No.4

Veg Patch
by Mark Diacono
introduced by Hugh Fearnley-Whittingstall

River Cottage Handbook No.5

Edible Seashore
by John Wright
introduced by Hugh Fearnley-Whittingstall

River Cottage Handbook No.6

Sea Fishing
by Nick Fisher
introduced by Hugh Fearnley-Whittingstall

River Cottage Handbook No.7

Hedgerow
by John Wright
introduced by Hugh Fearnley-Whittingstall

River Cottage Handbook No.8

Cakes
by Pam Corbin
introduced by Hugh Fearnley-Whittingstall

River Cottage Handbook No.9

Fruit
by Mark Diacono
introduced by Hugh Fearnley-Whittingstall

River Cottage Handbook No.10

Herbs
by Nikki Duffy
introduced by Hugh Fearnley-Whittingstall

River Cottage Handbook No.11

Chicken & Eggs
by Mark Diacono
introduced by Hugh Fearnley-whittingstall

River Cottage Handbook No.12

Booze
by John Wright
introduced by Hugh Fearnley-Whittingstall

Seasonal, Local, Organic, Wild

FOR FURTHER INFORMATION AND
TO ORDER ONLINE, VISIT
RIVERCOTTAGE.NET